Galaxy

Galaxy

THE HEALING POWERS OF A RESCUE DOG

JEN WILSON and Judy Katz

Essex, Connecticut

An imprint of The Globe Pequot Publishing Group, Inc.
64 South Main Street
Essex, CT 06426
www.globepequot.com

Copyright © 2026 by Jen Wilson

All rights reserved. No part of this book may be reproduced in any form or by any electronic or mechanical means, including information storage and retrieval systems, without written permission from the publisher, except by a reviewer who may quote passages in a review.

British Library Cataloguing in Publication Information available

Library of Congress Cataloging-in-Publication Data available

ISBN 9781493093083 (paperback) | ISBN 9781493093090 (epub)

Contents

Prologue vii

CHAPTER ONE 1
CHAPTER TWO 21
CHAPTER THREE 31
CHAPTER FOUR 39
CHAPTER FIVE 47
CHAPTER SIX 55
CHAPTER SEVEN 65
CHAPTER EIGHT 77
CHAPTER NINE 81
CHAPTER TEN 89
CHAPTER ELEVEN 95
CHAPTER TWELVE 105
CHAPTER THIRTEEN 113
CHAPTER FOURTEEN 123
CHAPTER FIFTEEN 131
CHAPTER SIXTEEN 139
CHAPTER SEVENTEEN 145
CHAPTER EIGHTEEN 155
CHAPTER NINETEEN 167
CHAPTER TWENTY 173
CHAPTER TWENTY-ONE 179

Meet the Authors 183

Prologue

THE ROOM WAS DARKENED. FROM THE DOORWAY, I COULD BARELY MAKE out the man sitting in the wheelchair beside the bed. But his mood came off palpably, in toxic waves of angry heat. The medical staff said he wasn't talking to anyone. He was recently back from Afghanistan, minus both his legs and some fingers on one hand. He was twenty-five years old.

The nurse who had brought us to visit him went to his side and asked if the dog could come in. He slowly nodded assent but still said nothing. I led Galaxy in. That's all she was waiting for. Without hesitation, she ran over to his side, put her muzzle on his lap, and looked up at him. The man and the dog locked eyes. They stayed like that, wordless and motionless. Time stood still. What seemed like forever turned out to be only minutes.

When it was time to leave, I called Galaxy. She gave the patient one last look and walked out of his room. That was the beginning of a transformation—and a journey—I could not have imagined. Unbeknown to me, this unusual, complicated dog that had come into my family's life would, in an odd way, change so much for us and everyone around her. Galaxy had a rare gift of healing others, born out of her pain. In subsequent visits, she would transform this soldier's life and the lives of many others who urgently needed her type of connection and acceptance—a type of unconditional love that humans have been getting from dogs for millennia. For me, in this new world of certified therapy dogs we were entering, that was a beginning I could not have imagined when my son begged my husband and me to go with him to the local shelter and adopt a dog.

Chapter One

They say you never adopt the dog you *want*. You adopt the dog you *need*. I didn't think I needed a dog. I'd grown up with them and loved dogs, but I didn't feel like anything was missing from my life without a dog. My husband, son, and I were a happy family, living in the warm golden desert of Las Vegas, Nevada. Sometimes the universe has other plans. Sometimes an unexpected gift can change *everything*—every part of your life, how you see yourself, and how you see everything and everyone else around you. Sometimes fate, or God, or the universe, or maybe even just a happy accident, has a way of giving you something that touches every part of your life, changes everything, turning everything it touches into gold. Such is the surprise the universe had in store when my son Aaron began pleading for a dog.

"Mommy, Daddy, can we get a dog?"

Our son was four years old the first time we heard that. We held out for two whole years, telling him no.

"A dog is a lot of responsibility."

"A dog requires a lot of time and attention."

"Dogs need discipline and hard work."

Every justification we could think of, we gave him. But for the next two years, he kept asking. I have no idea where he could have gotten that stubborn streak. Must be from his father's side. Then, right after his sixth birthday, I was perusing the internet randomly, and up popped a special "empty the shelter" adoption event held that weekend by one of the local animal shelters in town. They were waiving all adoption and spay/neuter fees.

I showed it to my husband, Alan. "Babe, look at this."

He looked. "Oh, that's a good deal."

"Aaron's been hounding us for a dog for so long. Want to at least take a look?"

He was hesitant. His only experience with owning dogs had been a childhood Akita with some significant aggression and behavioral problems. It certainly wasn't the type of pet he was eager to have around his very young son. "I don't know a lot about dogs. Don't rescues generally have some problems?"

"Sometimes, but not always."

"Well, you're the dog person. As long as you pick the dog and make sure there are no big red flags, I'm good with it."

So that weekend we went to the crowded shelter. We got there early, but all the small dogs were already gone. We walked through the shelter, looking at all the excited dogs barking in their kennels. Aaron found one, a very sweet and playful pittie terrier mix named Puzzle. She was extremely friendly and outgoing, eagerly licking us through the front spokes of her kennel. Alan went to find an employee to get her out.

While Aaron and I waited, we walked down the rest of the row. There, at the end, was another dog. The sign on her kennel said she was an American Bully, was three years old, and that her name was Muse.

Chapter One

Much larger than pittie terrier Puzzle, she was more stocky and had oddly chopped ears. What caught my attention was the fact that she wasn't barking or jumping like the others. She also wasn't cowering in the far corner like some of the more troubled dogs. She was lying quietly and calmly at the front of her kennel.

She looked up at us as we approached, but other than that she didn't react. The shelter had bags of treats that guests could give dogs, so I knelt and offered her one through the kennel door. The promise of food perked her up, her tail started wagging, and she sat up to take it gently from my hand. When she looked at me, and our eyes met, the connection was instant. We decided to pull her out instead of Puzzle.

She was assertive, had obviously never been on a leash before, and didn't seem to understand human boundaries. Her obvious strength, stocky build, and the fact that she all but dragged the shelter employee behind her as he led us all to one of the socialization runs made Alan nervous. This was seventy pounds of solid muscle, sharp teeth, and no real understanding of human rules. She was friendly but had no concept of boundaries or personal space.

But what stood out to me was just how ungodly quiet and calm she was. No jumping, no barking, and no apparent dominance or aggression issues.

At one point, while I was holding the leash in the crowded socialization pen, she got into Aaron's space, wanting attention and not understanding the fact that she outweighed the six-year-old boy by twenty pounds. Aaron was slightly intimidated, stepping backward and turning away. I immediately popped the leash, paired with a stern, "Hey."

It was a mild correction, mostly just to judge how responsive this dog was, and I was delighted to see that she immediately backed off. I gave her a larger jerky treat to test for resource guarding, then took it away. She didn't mind at all. She was just so mellow and laid-back.

Alan quickly became more comfortable with her, too. Even though she was still a very large and powerful dog, he could see how mellow and low energy she was, how friendly and affectionate she was, and how eager she was to please. The longer he interacted with her, the more he saw her personality, and the more relaxed he became. He'd said the final decision would be mine, but this was every bit mutual. It was clear we'd found the perfect dog for us. We took her home and renamed her Galaxy.

Like most rescue dogs, we knew nothing about her. We did know that she'd been in the shelter for a few weeks and had been captured and taken there as a stray. They spayed her in the shelter. Her records showed that she was fearful of the shelter vet but allowed him to perform his exams. She was nervous inside the house at first. It was clear that she had never really been an indoor dog. She had no understanding of boundaries inside a human home.

I grew up here in Las Vegas but on the outskirts of town, maybe five miles from "The Strip." When I was young, we had horses and a decent patch of land, and we spent our time going to horse competitions. We always had working dogs: Australian Cattle Dogs, Australian and German Shepherds—even a puppy we rescued thinking she was a German Shepherd that ended up being half German Shepherd and half Doberman. I loved them all. The Doberman mix was my best friend through my teen years. But Galaxy, she was different. I had never had a dog like her before. All our dogs were more independent than clingy. Galaxy is a "Velcro" dog, both clingy *and* attentive, all the time.

What was so helpful in those early days was my familiarity and comfort with dogs. I know how to train them, and Galaxy proved to be very easy to train. Once she understood that chewing on shoes and jumping on the bed were both off-limits, she was content to stay within those boundaries. Within a week, she was perfect. *Inside* the house.

Outside and around other people, she was a nervous wreck. Barking, running away, shaking, trembling. The fearfulness mentioned in her file at the shelter was more than simply nervousness due to unfamiliar surroundings. It was an all-encompassing part of her psyche. She seemed convinced that the world was a scary place and that everything would eat her. She was fearful and neurotic with friends, relatives, and everyone else. She had weird little quirks, too. She was terrified of squeaky toys, her dog bed, car rides, and iPhone ringtones. It was sad to watch. She was gentle and calm, but the most minor thing would send her cowering in the corner of my bedroom, trembling and whimpering. I started to suspect that she'd been abused.

Chapter One

It came to a head when we took her to her first vet appointment. She was okay with the vet techs, but as soon as the doctor walked in, she started screaming—not barking, *screaming*. She tried to hide all her seventy pounds under my chair. When the doctor tried to move her into the back room for blood work, she got so worked up that she vomited. That was a big red flag to me. This was more than just timidity and shyness. This was pure fear and red-zone panic. I knew we had to do something. I'd seen enough fearful dogs to know they eventually stop barking and start biting. I also knew that the prejudice and fear of pit bulls and bully breeds were still going on. I'd never met a pit I didn't like, but still, I wasn't necessarily over the moon about pit bull–type breeds either. I always preferred the shepherds and cattle dogs.

We got Galaxy because she was calm, not because of her breed. But now I had a terrified, utterly psychotic pit bull dog, right in the middle of the pit bull hysteria. This was a headline waiting to happen.

Alan was unsure about what to do. He already loved her and had bonded with her, but he had so little experience with dogs, which was a significant problem. A potentially *dangerous* problem, given Galaxy's size and strength. Even I had to admit that this kind of fear was over my head. I'd never heard a dog scream like that before. I'd never seen a dog just frantically panicking like that.

We didn't want to surrender her because she was so well behaved and polite with us. She already loved us and had already started showing more of her real personality. She was still calm with us, still mellow and gentle, still great with Aaron.

In the house, she was perfectly behaved. As I said, she quickly learned the boundaries and became comfortable operating within them. While she was clumsy and not used to living indoors, which led to her constantly knocking things over or bumping into things, she had this gentleness that took me by surprise. Her eagerness to please was also extraordinary. I'd never seen a dog as "owner centric" as she was. She wanted to do whatever it took to make us happy with her.

In less than a week, she was wholly housetrained. She knew which toys were hers and which were Aaron's. She knew what could be chewed on and what couldn't. She also knew which furniture she could lie on and which she couldn't. As deeply food oriented as she is, she still begged but knew to keep a respectful distance while people were eating.

I believe there are five "tricks" every dog needs to know to keep them and everyone around them safe. I call them "The Big Five": their name, "come," "sit/stay," "leave it," and "drop it." These are commands that keep dogs safe, particularly in a big city or—in my case, when the dogs I had growing up spent time around two-thousand-pound animals with sharp teeth and hooves.

Teaching them to know their name is easy, and their name should only ever be used for good things—never used to punish or scold a dog. When a dog hears their name, they should immediately perk up and look at you. It should mean that good things are coming. Their name should be one of their favorite sounds in the world.

Even when there are a lot of other things going on, or if the dog is exploring a new area full of fascinating new smells to discover, calling their name should be a surefire way to get their attention back on you.

The "come" command is another important lesson or "trick." Again, it should only be used positively. A dog should never be scolded for coming to you, even if it was doing something terrible just before. Imagine you're on a crowded city street and your dog somehow slipped out of its collar and is now darting toward oncoming traffic. The word *come* needs to be even more exciting than whatever the dog is running toward. The dog should be thrilled to run back to its owner.

"Leave it" is probably one of the most important commands to teach a dog. You want to be able to communicate to your dog that the mysterious puddle of goo on the ground—or the dead rodent, or your favorite shoes, or the neighbor's cat, or whatever has distracted him or her—might be incredibly tempting, but the dog needs to leave it alone. Teaching your dog to "leave it" means that you don't have to worry as much about spilled antifreeze in the garage, a dropped clove of garlic in the kitchen, or a forgotten bag of Halloween candy your kid hid under their bed.

But what if you were too late, and the dog already has the dead rodent/clove of garlic/your expensive shoe in its mouth? That's where "drop it" comes in. Aside from keeping your dog safe from ingesting something dangerous, it also helps avoid problems with resource guarding.

Within a week, Galaxy had mastered "come," "sit/stay," and her name. She was well on her way to mastering "leave it" and "drop it." She was remarkably easy to train, despite not being quite on the same level intellectually as my Doberman mix and my Red Heeler. Even if she didn't understand what I was asking her, she was always very motivated to figure out what I wanted and how to make me happy.

I was used to training independent, eerily intelligent dogs on how to do complex tasks around horses and cattle. Galaxy wasn't intelligent in the way that my shepherds and cattle dogs were, but she seemed to have an emotional intelligence that I'd never seen before in a dog. As she became more comfortable with us, and more of her personality started to show, however, she also became the most clingy dog I've ever had—by far. In her mind, there was no such thing as too much attention and affection. She was never particularly exuberant or playful, but she'd spend hours lying in my lap, shoving her nose under my hand to urge me to pet her. Whenever Alan came up to hug me or kiss me or show any kind of affection, Galaxy would come right up and sit down right in front of us, staring expectantly up at us, her tail wagging, waiting for her turn. That quickly became a game that still gets played to this day. Every time Alan hugs me, every time he reaches to caress me or touch me, Galaxy is sitting patiently right there, waiting for him to pet her. No one in our house is allowed to hug anyone else without also loving on the dog.

With Aaron, she was fantastic, incredibly gentle and sweet. As big as she was, it took her a matter of days to learn that the tiny human was fragile and that she needed to be more mindful. She tended to move more slowly around Aaron, and while she still enjoyed resting her head in Aaron's lap, she wasn't as demanding of his attention as she was with us. She learned very quickly that tiny humans require extra carefulness, and both Alan and I were impressed with how gentle Galaxy was with our six-year-old.

With everyone else, though, she was terrified. A complete neurotic mess. Our relatives and friends couldn't even go into the backyard when she was there without her constantly barking in a high, squeaky, petrified voice. She'd stand just a few feet away from them, just out of reach, constantly barking. Whenever delivery people or the yard maintenance guys

Chapter One

came here, we had to keep her inside. Taking her anywhere in public was out of the question. The sight of other people and dogs stressed her to the point that she'd become completely manic, pulling on the leash and barking in that same high squeaky voice.

I'd never seen a dog *this* terrified of everything. In Galaxy's mind, the world was a dangerous, cruel place, with everything and everyone in it eager to hurt her. She would get herself so stressed out that she'd start shaking, and nothing we could do would calm her down. We realized we didn't have the knowledge or experience to help her by ourselves. We needed help. This was kind of a blow to my ego, honestly. Again, I grew up with dogs. I knew how to communicate complex tasks and ideas to my dogs, even from a distance, while on the back of a horse, with a whole lot else going on. I was good at it. I saw my dogs not as my babies or pets but as my partners. I respected their judgment and their instincts, and they respected my leadership.

I'd rescued German Shepherds, Australian Shepherds, and German Shepherd mixes, and the shelter mutts were always just as capable, intelligent, and profoundly bonded to me as our purebred dogs. I am an experienced and knowledgeable dog owner. I know what I'm doing. Before moving in with Alan, I had two decades of experience. But seeing Galaxy like that, any shred of rationality shut down by fear, was a wake-up call. Her fear screamed in her mind, drowning out everything else. This was dangerous. We had to do *something*. Doing nothing wasn't an option.

We didn't want to take her back to the shelter because she was so good with us and had already settled into her new life as part of our family. She was flawlessly housetrained within a few days and, again, very quickly had a solid grasp of what is and is not allowed in our house. She was happy with us, and we were happy with her. We didn't want to have to give her up because of her fear. But we had to address the problem, or her fear would only get worse.

So I turned to the internet, looking for dog trainers in my area. I happened across one site called "Peace, Love, and Pit Bulls." Well, that sounded perfect. I messaged the owner, and he responded within the hour. He told me his name was Tino. We had an appointment to meet in a public park later that week. Even the idea of meeting in a park had me apprehensive. Galaxy was scared of *everything*. New people, other dogs, new places, it didn't matter. The entire world was terrifying.

How would I even be able to get her there? And Alan was apprehensive about the cost. "That seems like a lot for a dog trainer," he told me.

"I don't know. I've never needed to hire a trainer before. But what are our options? Take her back to the shelter?"

He visibly recoiled from the idea. "No, I don't want to do that."

"Tino said the first consultation would be free. We won't lose anything by letting him take a look at her. If we don't like what he says, we can just leave."

He nodded. "That's fair."

The day of our consultation came. We loaded a very anxious dog into the back of the car and headed to the park, with Galaxy whining and pacing in the back the entire way. We got there shortly before Tino did. He told us where he'd meet us, and we waited together, with Galaxy constantly pacing on her leash. I tried talking to her to calm her down. Alan even tried kneeling on the grass next to her to try and distract her from how anxious she was. Nothing helped, and she just kept pacing. After a few minutes, Tino pulled up and got out of his car. Also coming out of the car was a very handsome, chunky bulldog mix. No leash. The dog was incredibly calm and steady. He didn't pay attention to other people or dogs and focused entirely on his owner.

Tino greeted both of us, then turned his attention to Galaxy. "All right. Is she protective of you at all?"

"Honestly, I can't tell. She's just scared of everything."

"Let me take her and walk over here. She might be a little better behaved if she's not right next to you."

I handed him her leash, and he started leading her away. But as soon as Galaxy realized that a strange man was holding her leash, she freaked out. She began barking and growling nonstop, even as he encouraged her to follow him. That high-pitched, panicked bark was back, and she yanked desperately on the leash, trying to get away. When she realized she couldn't get away, she stood there, at the end of her leash, just far enough away that he couldn't reach her if he tried to touch her, and barked. What struck me the most, as I watched him, was how calm he

Chapter One

was. I was sure it had to be intimidating to have a big dog that intense barking so much at him, but he wasn't afraid or nervous. He stood there with her, calmly waiting her out until she stopped to sniff his foot.

His calm demeanor was beyond reassuring for me. He wasn't intimidated; he wasn't scared. He just waited her out as if nothing was wrong. Only a few seconds had passed, and I knew he would be our trainer.

"I use an e-collar," he explained. "I'm going to put it on her now."

"Go for it," I told him. I didn't know anything about e-collars. I had never used them, but everything about this man was reassuring and calming. Watching how he reacted to Galaxy's fear and aggression, it was clear he knew what he was doing. If he thought an e-collar could help her, I immediately believed him. He bent down and gave Galaxy some affection, then strapped the collar onto her, all while explaining to me how to use it.

For those who have never heard of an e-collar, let me explain. It's an electric collar with a remote that will deliver either a vibration or a shock to get Galaxy's attention. You're supposed to start at setting 0 and slowly move up until the dog notices and looks at you, and that's the dog's control setting.

"Let her be the one to tell you what she needs," Tino told us. "You always start at the lowest setting and never go higher than they need."

I was in awe as I watched him work with her. He pressed a button on the remote, and suddenly, in an instant Galaxy's fear seemed to disappear. She calmly followed him, focused on him just like his own dog. Even when he abruptly changed directions, challenging her to remain focused on him, she *still* followed. There was none of her apparent fear or screaming, nor the panic she'd first exhibited when he'd taken her leash from me and stepped away. Her hackles had lowered, and she was a completely different dog.

"Has she had e-collar training before?" he asked us.

"I have no idea."

"I think she must have. This is incredible. She already knows just what to do."

He changed direction again, and again she turned and followed him without him needing to pull on the leash.

Chapter One

He chuckled softly. "This dog, man. This is such a good dog!"

I was stunned and speechless.

This was the same dog that had *screamed* in utter terror at the vet. That had whimpered and paced in the back of the car only ten minutes ago, on the way to the park. That had whined constantly and had been nothing but anxious and agitated while we waited for Tino to arrive. This was the same dog that had barked fearfully at him, hackles raised and teeth bared, only a minute ago.

"Look at this," he said, walking up to show me the remote. "She's on level 8."

"Is that good?"

"That's the intensity. It's 8 out of 100."

"Out of *100*?" I asked, shocked. "You saw her! You saw how terrified she was. That was all it took?"

He grinned at me. "That's all it took. This is such a good dog."

Alan and I exchanged looks as Tino began working with her again, walking her away from us. This *was* a completely different dog. She was calm. Relaxed. No hint of fear or anxiety.

"I think we need to hire him," I whispered.

"Yeah, dammit, I think we do, too."

I laughed. "'Dammit'?"

He shrugged and smiled at me. "You know me. I hate to spend money. But yeah, this is a big change. We've got to hire him."

Tino finished working with Galaxy and walked back over to us. "There's nothing here that can't be fixed," he told us. "She's fearful and timid, so we've got to work on building her confidence. I'll show you what to do with her, and if you decide you want to do sessions, we'll get her over her fear."

He looked down at her and smiled. "But you've got such a great dog here. She must have had training before. This is just awesome."

We hired him, and under his guidance, we were able to work through some of her biggest fears. After only a couple of weeks, she was calm enough that she could handle a vet exam. We took her back to the vet. They did the exam, blood work, and a couple of X-rays, and we learned some things—namely, that my suspicions were correct. This wasn't a case of neglect or abandonment but outright abuse.

Her ears were crooked and jagged because they weren't cropped by a vet under anesthesia but, horrifically, cut off with a pair of scissors when she was a puppy. The vet told us he could always tell because one side doesn't look too bad, but the puppy is struggling and in excruciating pain, so the second ear is always uneven. Even though she was only three or four years old, she'd already been bred multiple times. Her jaw had been broken, and her trachea collapsed. She'd been stabbed. Twice.

They X-rayed her back legs because she seemed to have some stiffness and discovered that they'd both been deliberately broken and were never set correctly. She had bad knees and would eventually need surgery. But because the treatment and recovery are so brutal, they only do it when the pain is severe enough to affect the dog's quality of life. Galaxy wasn't there yet, so we got joint health supplements and prescription dog food for mobility and joint health.

Finding all that out, seeing the irreparable damage done to her, the unimaginable cruelty she endured, and the pain she was still in, was heartbreaking. All her fear suddenly made sense. This was such a good dog. She loved us, and once she got comfortable with Tino, she loved him, too. He even posted on his social media that dogs like her are the reason he loves his job and the reason why he does what he does. She was scared of everything but eager to please, and she seemed to have an innate ability to understand what humans want from her.

She *wanted* to be a good dog. She tried to make us happy. After only a few weeks of owning her, it seemed that her entire world revolved around us. All she ever wanted was to be close to us, to snuggle with us, and to lay her giant blocky head on our laps. She didn't deserve what had been done to her. She didn't deserve the cruelty that left her so fearful and anxious. She didn't deserve the pain that would haunt her every day for the rest of her life.

I felt sorry for her. I wanted to spoil her with love and attention to compensate for her torture. But Tino was very clear. We could *not* feel sorry for her. We could *not* let her get away with anything because of her past trauma. He helped us understand how to work with her in a way

Chapter One

that was helpful to *her*, rather than what made us feel better. Spoiling her now would make us feel better but would only confuse her. We had to adapt to how she thinks and learn to communicate with her in a way she could easily understand. Which, logically, I agree with. I know dogs' minds don't work like ours, and that they process trauma differently than we do. Still, it was a struggle at first to continue being sympathetic while guiding her out from that fearful, neurotic headspace she was lost in.

He taught us how to use the e-collar, and we began the process of slowly, gradually working through her fears. As time passed and Galaxy started improving, I became less vigilant about using the e-collar quite the way Tino suggested—mostly because she didn't need it. Her control level was so low, so mild, that it was barely worth using. I relied much more on the vibration than the electrical setting. Usually, a quick, sharp "Hey" was enough to snap her out of it when she'd get lost in a manic episode. The vibration also didn't carry nearly the controversy of the e-collar itself.

Some already judged me for having a pit bull, or at least having a dog people saw as pit-bull adjacent. Also, some people think e-collars are meant to punish or hurt dogs. I usually show them I'm not hurting Galaxy by taking the collar off and letting them see how she reacts to me putting it back on. She wouldn't want to wear it if it hurt her. I use the vibration setting only when she sees a small animal that sets off her prey drive, or another dog walks up to us, or when she's at the vet, and her fear starts making her frantic. There's no shock—it just vibrates, but it breaks her out of those obsessive mental processes and helps keep her calm when she gets scared.

I think now that she sees it as kind of a security blanket. When I'm not using it, I keep it on the charger and literally cannot touch it or take it off its charger without her getting excited and following me around: she knows that collar means she's going to go somewhere fun. Not work, though. She wasn't allowed to wear it at work—a development we will get to shortly.

It took lots and lots of positive reinforcement to help build her confidence, rigid consistency with rules and boundaries to help her feel more secure, and teaching her to look to me when she's nervous (i.e., if I'm calm, she should be calm, too). In truth, it was exhausting. Once we'd mastered putting her in a calm headspace at home, we started taking her out in public. Of course, she had missed out on crucial puppy socialization, so it took some time to work her through her fears of the world. Even when she was relatively calm, being approached by someone she didn't know would still scare her. Depending on how assertive the person's energy was, she'd either move to stand behind me or growl at the person.

Luckily, she was always highly motivated by both food and affection. One day, after weeks of constant work and frustration, she finally seemed to understand that most new people would stop to give her affection if she was sweet and friendly. Once she figured that out, her fear of new people disappeared overnight, and she turned her focus to figuring out how to convince the person to pet her. Her fear of the mailman, delivery drivers, and yard maintenance guys was completely gone in a relatively short period. It had taken time, but she got better.

I decided to work toward having Galaxy pass the Canine Good Citizen (CGC) test from the American Kennel Club (AKC). It's a test that the AKC offers to help dogs learn good manners and basic commands, and it's a prerequisite for many more advanced programs, such as becoming a therapy dog. It could also offer a small degree of protection if we become victims of unfair prejudice or accusations. A CGC title shows that a dog was evaluated and tested by an accredited evaluator and was determined to be safe and well behaved in public.

Upon passing, Galaxy received a certificate from the AKC. Her title gives us the right to add the letters *CGC* behind her name on her ID tags and any official records at the vet, boarders, groomers, and such, as well as being added to her official AKC registered name. I have to admit I like being able to brag about it. It's not a difficult test to pass, it just feels *fancy* to be able to introduce her as "Galaxy, CGC."

That was such a proud moment for all of us. It was more than just a piece of paper, more than just a certificate, but concrete proof of how much she'd grown and how far she'd come. For us, it was recognition for our hard work, and for all the work *she* put in learning to trust us to take care of her and keep her safe.

After we got her through her biggest fears, she was a completely different dog. She was happy and outgoing. Her fear of other people was gone entirely. With every new person, she met a potential best friend. She went with us to all the places where dogs were allowed. Hiking, parks, dog-friendly stores, and restaurants—she came with us everywhere. Wherever she went, she always attracted *a lot* of attention. Which, of course, she loved.

People would often stop us to compliment her on how beautiful she was. As soon as they started talking to her, she would happily approach them, her tail wagging, her butt wiggling, moving to stand sideways

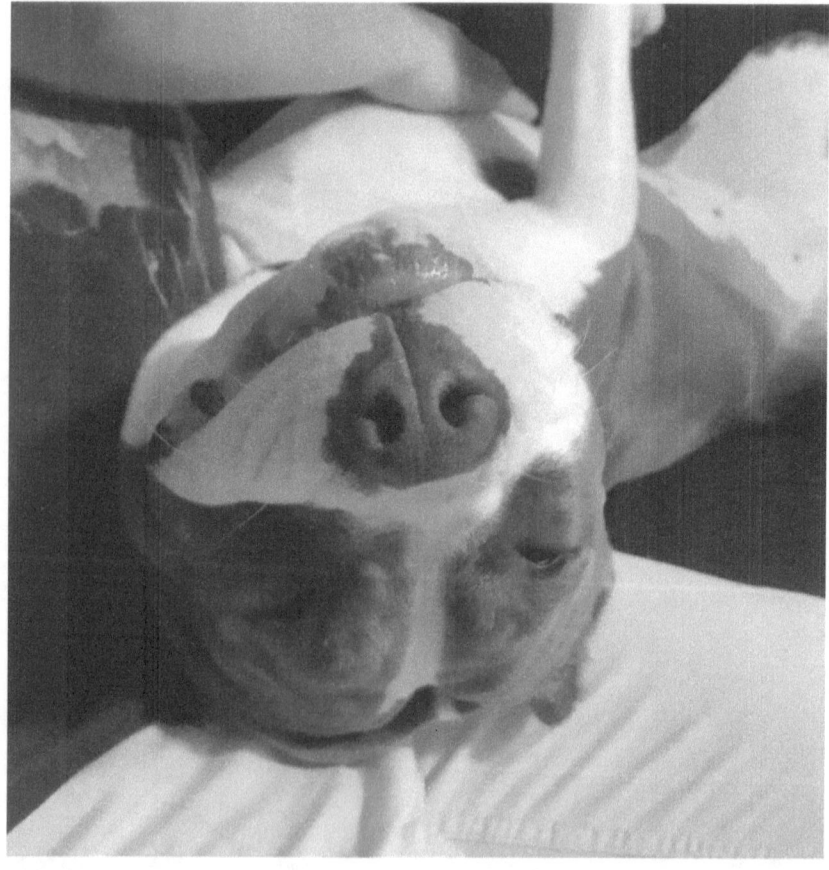

Chapter One

against them so she could lean all seventy pounds against their legs while they'd pet her entire body. She even learned the phrase, "Is she friendly?"

Usually, when she's out with us, she is expected to remain at my left side, in a perfect heel, until she hears her release word. But she learned that when someone asks, "Is she friendly?" it means she's about to be spoiled with attention, so she started leaving my side without the release word, walking toward them so they could pet her.

It was funny. I knew I *should* retrain her not to respond to that question. But honestly, it was too cute to correct. I never tell anyone they can't pet her, and she knows she's supposed to stay at a heel every other time, so I let it slide. Every time it happened, I couldn't help but grin because she took it upon herself to learn what that phrase meant, and hearing it always made her happy.

This dog that had overcome such pain, abuse, and cruelty was now happily enjoying all the good the world has to offer. Once the training for her CGC title was done, however, I was surprised to discover that I felt a little disappointed. I *enjoyed* working with her. I loved all our training and socialization sessions, and I didn't want it to end. So I started thinking about what I was going to do with her next. I considered a few different options, but nothing really jumped out at me, and her joint problems limited our options even further. As it turned out, though, Galaxy knew what she wanted to do, and one day she showed me. It was a day, a moment, that would change my life, and the way I saw her, forever.

Chapter Two

I WAS STILL A RELATIVELY NEW OWNER OF A DOG MOST PEOPLE OUTSIDE the dog world considered a pit bull but already found it difficult to fit in with the pit bull advocate crowd. Even among pittie owners, there doesn't seem to be any clear consensus on what a pit bull *is*. Some insist that only the American Pit Bull Terrier can be called a pit bull. But an American Pit Bull Terrier (APBT), colloquially called an APB, is only recognized as its breed by the UKC, or United Kennel Club, and the American Dog Breeders Association. The American Kennel Club does not recognize it. No American organization recognizes the APBT as a breed. As such, American Pit Bull Terriers are relatively rare in the United States. Most dogs labeled as "pit bulls" here in the United States are American Staffordshire Terriers or Staffordshire Bull Terriers. Other pit bull advocates will include those two similar breeds in their description of pit bulls.

Thus, those three breeds—the American Pit Bull Terrier, American Staffordshire Terrier, and the Staffordshire Bull Terrier—are generally considered the three standard "pittie" breeds. Other people in the field will also include Bull Terriers and American Bullies like Galaxy. Yet others will include larger "Molosser" dogs like mastiffs, American Bulldogs, and Boxers. That term, *Molosser*, was new to me. I looked it up and learned that there once was a breed of large, solidly built "bulldogs"—dogs called Molossers because they came from the Molossia area of Ancient Greece. Today's American Bully dogs combine the muscle power and tenacity of those bulldogs with the alertness, agility, and speed of the original British terrier.

I realized early on that my understanding and opinions didn't matter to many people. The world saw Galaxy's muscular and solid build, giant blocky head, and chopped ears and decided she was a pit bull. It didn't matter that she outweighed the largest American Pit Bull Terrier, American Staffordshire Terrier, and Staffordshire Bull Terrier by a lot. It didn't matter that most pit bulls are agile and athletic, while Galaxy prances around with all the grace of a drunken elephant. Petco, Delta Airlines, the vet, our HOA, the boarders, the press, the media, and everyone who meets her have all decided she's a pit bull, and I didn't see the need to nitpick. I became very comfortable calling her a pit bull and thinking of her that way.

This ruffled the feathers of some pit bull advocates and owners of American Pit Bull Terriers, so I never felt like I could belong to that community; I struggled to find a place where Galaxy and I could feel like we belonged. Many people adored her, and she loved the attention she drew everywhere she went, but others were less welcoming.

I couldn't blame them, not really. Galaxy is a *big* girl with a big head; large, strong jaws; sharp teeth; and chopped ears. She intimidates a lot of people. Sometimes that limits where we can go and what we can do with her. We still brought her everywhere with us. Her first Halloween with us was especially fun, though I don't think she was a big fan of her Yoda ears costume. No accounting for taste, I suppose.

Interestingly enough, I didn't know what an American Bully *was* until I got her. I just assumed it was an American Bulldog. Galaxy was shorter and stockier than most American Bulldogs, but I assumed that was just a product of her being mixed with something else, as is the case with most rescue dogs. I never really paid attention to what actual breed she might be. It wasn't until we had her out with us at a park, and a man stopped to compliment her, that I learned there was a difference.

"That's a beautiful dog, man," he said.

Alan and I smiled, and Aaron piped up and said, "Her name is Galaxy. She's friendly."

The man approached to pet her. As he did, I could see him looking up and down her body. "Oh, yeah, she's a good-looking dog. She's a Got, right?"

"A what?"

"A Gotti? She's a Gotti line, isn't she?"

I looked at Alan in confusion. "I don't know what that is."

Alan agreed. "She's a rescue. We don't know what she is."

"Oh, she *looks* like a Gotti. Here, take a look."

He pulled up pictures on his cell phone to show us. Sure enough, we found ourselves looking at a very handsome, distinguished-looking stud that seemed eerily similar to Galaxy.

"Oh, wow!" I exclaimed, taking his phone to get a better look. "That *does* look like her!"

"Yeah, they're some great dogs."

"But what are they? What is a Gotti, exactly?"

"It's a bloodline. One of the most famous American Bully bloodlines."

"She's a shelter mutt, but her breed paperwork said she was an American Bully. I just assumed it was a bully mix."

He shook his head. "No. They sound similar, but the American Bully is a separate breed. They're still kind of new. I think the UKC only recently recognized them as a distinct breed in . . . 2013. They've kind of exploded in popularity since then. Gotti is one of the best. You sure she's not a Gotti?"

I looked at the picture on his phone. "Gottis are expensive, right?"

"Big time."

I shrugged. "She was an abused rescue. I can't imagine anyone spending that kind of money on a dog like that just to turn around and treat it the way she was treated."

"Maybe one of her parents was a Gotti," Alan supplied.

But I wasn't convinced. "Even if that were the case, the puppies would be valuable. A puppy like that, you wouldn't chop their ears off with scissors. You'd take them to a vet to be cropped under anesthesia."

The man nodded his head in agreement. "Yeah, that's a good point. It's not just the money; it's the status. Gotti pups have a waiting list. You don't just get one and do something like that to it. That's a fucked-up thing to do in any case." He knelt back down to pet Galaxy again. "So you're just naturally a good-looking lady, aren't you? You don't need a fancy pedigree or bloodline; you've got it all, girl."

I thanked him and quickly went home to research American Bullies. I had to laugh. This whole time, I'd completely dismissed it when

Chapter Two

they said she was an "American Bully." In my ignorance, I thought that description was just another way of saying she was a "backyard-bred mutt who looks like a buff pit bull." At that point, I had no idea that they were referring to a specific breed.

While we thought Galaxy might still be a backyard-bred mutt, both her appearance and temperament seemed to fit extraordinarily well with the American Bully: annoyingly clingy, uncompromisingly loyal, and friendly to a fault. I even remember reading that, despite their intimidating, tank-like appearance and giant, blocky heads and powerful jaws, they are *not* recommended for guard dogs or protection dogs, simply because they're not reliably aggressive enough toward people. They still may be prone to dog reactivity, as most pit bull and bully breeds are, but American Bullies are so friendly and people oriented that even a dog-reactive Bully would just be too friendly with humans to be an effective guard dog.

And yeah, that fit Galaxy to a *T*. Once she'd gotten past her fears, she was just too friendly with every person and wanted nothing but to be petted by any human who got close. A potential burglar might see her running around in the backyard and choose not to take his chances with such an intimidating-looking dog. But the reality was that if someone were to break in here and talk to her, she'd happily run up to greet him and follow him around, tail wagging, begging for pets, as he stole everything we owned.

It was amusing to me that the only reason I knew anything about her breed, or American Bullies at all, was because a random stranger saw Galaxy and thought she was some fancy elite lady who cost us thousands of dollars rather than the backyard-bred mutt we assumed she was. But I'd gotten used to people, particularly men, stopping to compliment me on her beauty. I liked that. I liked it even more when I'd see these giant, intimidating mountains of muscle and tattoos crouch down to cuddle my dog. I liked it even more when I heard those gruff, deep voices go much higher whenever they talked to her. One massive, tall man giggled like a schoolgirl when he knelt to pet her, and Galaxy took that as an invitation to lick the skin off his face. It was the most adorable thing I'd seen in a very long time.

That was such a cool thing, one I'd never seen with any of my other dogs. Men seemed more comfortable cuddling with her than, say, a Cocker Spaniel or Yellow Lab, and Galaxy loved every minute of it. She'd eagerly trot up to even the scariest-looking man, her entire body wiggling, and just cuddle and lick him, no matter where we were or what else was happening. I loved watching it. I loved seeing a softer side to some of these big tough guys. Galaxy seemed to have a natural talent for bringing that softer side out in people, which was amazing. This was the same dog that had *screamed* in terror at the vet and would bark at anyone who got too close to her. This was the same dog that had been wholly petrified of every person in the world and would bark and snarl at them to keep them away.

But now there was none of that fear. She loved all people and only wanted them to love her. That in itself was amazing to me. That alone was something special. Her fear had been so profound and far-reaching, I'd wondered if she'd ever be able to get over it, but she surprised me. Her ability to let go of her fear gave her a completely new outlook on people and a new lease on life. She loved the attention, compliments, and random pets from strangers. So I was very used to the kind of attention she attracted everywhere she went, and I enjoyed it. I loved having her with me but still missed all of our training sessions and the time we devoted to working through her fears. I'll admit that I was feeling a little lost, and looking for direction. Then fate intervened, in the form of a single woman.

I never learned the woman's name, but to this day, I still remember her face and her voice. Those two things are forever burned into my memory. She was maybe in her fifties, or early sixties, with blonde hair that was curled and styled to frame her face. She was well dressed and petite. I only knew her for a few minutes. I only met her once, in passing, and never saw her again. But her impact on my life and Galaxy's life was utterly profound.

I had Galaxy out with me at the store about a month after her CGC test. I was still struggling to decide what I'd do with her next. In the store, a woman approached us in the aisle.

Chapter Two

"Your dog, she is beautiful. Very well behaved." Her voice was quiet, with a thick accent I couldn't quite place. I smiled and thanked her.

"She's very friendly. Would you like to pet her?"

The woman took a step back, smiling nervously. "Oh, no, I'm too afraid. I just wanted to tell you how beautiful she is. Very pleasant face. Very polite girl."

I thanked her for the compliment and told her how much I appreciated her telling me that, and then we went on with our shopping. Twice more, the same woman stopped me to compliment Galaxy. I asked her again if she'd like to pet her, and again she said she was too scared. She'd asked if I'd cropped her ears, and I explained that no, she'd been abused, and someone cut them off with scissors.

She gasped. "How horrible for someone to do that to such a kind creature!"

"Yeah, she had it rough for a while. But she's happy now, and she's our wonky-eared princess."

"Good that you saved her. She has a gentle face. I am scared to touch her, but she is a very beautiful girl. I am glad you give her a good life now."

She stopped me a third time while I was standing in line at the checkout. Finally, she confessed the reason for her fear. She pulled her hair back to reveal that her left ear had been completely mauled and shredded, long ago. Between the damage and the scar tissue, it was completely unrecognizable. She hid the scars on her face with makeup, but once she pointed them out, I could see them as well. She'd been attacked by a pit bull when she was a little girl.

My hand went to my mouth. I was stunned. I was heartbroken. This poor woman had lived through such a terrifying and traumatic event, and then she had to live with those scars, haunting her, reminding her of that fear and that pain, every time she looked in the mirror. She seemed like such a gentle woman, such a kind soul, but that pain just loomed over her.

"I'm so sorry that happened to you. It must have been so painful." It sounded silly, and I felt silly for saying it. But I didn't know what to say. I mean, what *can* you say to something like that? What could I possibly say? The pain that this woman has to carry with her is horrific. I can't even imagine what it must have been like for her, seeing the evidence of

Chapter Two

that attack on her face every single day. I wished I could say something to help her, to make her feel better, but there was nothing. She could never get away from it. It haunted her, and would always haunt her. After seeing that, I could understand her fear, and why she didn't want to touch Galaxy.

I was so focused on her that I didn't even notice Galaxy. But the woman looked down at her again and smiled. Then, without a word to me, she slowly, timidly, reached out a hand. I was expecting Galaxy to make her standard move, to stand up and approach the woman, like she always does when people pet her. For a split second, I was worried. If Galaxy did that, it would likely intimidate and scare the woman. She may not realize that Galaxy only wanted to be friendly. But Galaxy didn't move. She didn't stand up, and she didn't approach the woman; she stayed right there. As I watched her, looking up at that woman, everything about my dog changed. Her body language, expression, breathing, and even the way she held herself changed. If I had to put it into words, I'd describe it as *soft*. It was as if Galaxy deliberately made herself *softer*. Slower. Gentler. Every part of her body became relaxed, calm, and *soft*.

The woman put her hand on the top of Galaxy's head, running it over her chopped and jagged ears, lingering for a moment on what was left of her most jagged ear. "Someone hurt you, too, didn't they, little one?" After a moment, she moved to rest her hand on the side of Galaxy's head, and suddenly it seemed like the entire universe just clicked together.

I felt something I'd never felt before. It was like the rest of the store melted away. No one else and nothing else existed. It was just Galaxy, that woman, and the connection they were making. Galaxy was intensely focused on the woman. Gazing softly up at her, those calm almond-brown eyes met the woman's frightened, lonely blue ones. It had taken me *weeks* to train Galaxy to focus on me like that. But this woman, shut down by pain and fear, became Galaxy's entire world. She didn't move. She didn't look away. She just looked up, leaning her head just slightly against that woman's hand. It felt like Galaxy was saying to her, "I see you. I'm here. You're not alone."

In reality, I knew only a few seconds had passed, but it seemed as if time had slowed down. The outside world had disappeared. There was nothing else—nothing except these two tortured souls connecting. Galaxy knew exactly how to be. She knew, without needing me to tell her or train her, that getting up and approaching the woman would have only frightened her. She knew that this woman was hurting, and scared, but eager to love and show kindness. Galaxy seemed to know that she was healing just a tiny fraction of that woman's pain.

The look between them was beautiful. The moment seemed to stretch on, but Galaxy never wavered, never moved, never lost that focus. She reached into that woman's heart, through the fear and the pain, and settled around her soul. She gave her another soul to connect with.

The moment ended; the woman sighed, straightened up, and smiled at me, much brighter this time. "Very, very special girl." And then she walked away, leaving me standing there, with my jaw dropped, stunned silent. I didn't train Galaxy to do that. I didn't know something like that was even *possible*. What even *was* that? I looked down at Galaxy, still sitting on my left side. She lifted her head to look up at me.

"How in actual hell did you *do* that?" I asked her.

She wagged her tail and gave me a wide pittie grin.

"All right, so that's what we're going to do."

That was all I needed. She showed me what she could do, and she did it completely on her own, without being told or trained to do it. Galaxy showed me what she wanted to do with her life—what she wanted her life to mean—and I heard her, loud and clear. That night, when we got home, I looked up the therapy dog organizations in town and got her set up for all the testing and supervised visits she'd need. Now we had a direction. We had a focus. Galaxy decided that she had a job to do, and all she needed was the opportunity to do it.

Chapter Three

It didn't take long to get Galaxy ready for the therapy dog test, and the actual testing process took less than a half hour. She already had the basics down, and in any case, they were mostly screening more for temperament. Afterward, I would be paired with a woman who would oversee our supervised visits.

For our first visit, we went to a nursing home. I didn't know what to expect but was excited. That excitement ebbed a little, however, when I met Martina, the woman who was supposed to oversee our visits. When we pulled up, she was already waiting in the parking lot with her dog, Shelby. When I opened the back hatch of my SUV to reveal Galaxy standing there, waiting for me to set up the ramp she used to get out of the car, Martina took a step backward, pulling Shelby closer to her.

"Good morning," I said as I opened the back passenger door and pulled out Galaxy's ramp.

"The dogs need to be leashed," she told me.

I stopped. "Even in my car?"

"They need to be leashed for the entirety of the therapy session. It starts as soon as you get out of the car. Put a leash on the dog, please."

I set down the heavy plastic ramp and clipped Galaxy's leash to her collar.

"Take it easy," I whispered, half to Galaxy and half to myself. "Looks like it'll be one of *those* kinds of days." But Galaxy seemed utterly immune to the tension. She sat at the edge of the car, waiting patiently for her ramp, doing her silly pit bull grin.

I got the ramp in place and said, "Okay." Hearing her release word, Galaxy ran down the ramp. Martina took another step back.

"She needs to be under your complete control at all times." I bit back the urge to say something rude and instead looked straight at her.

"Heel," I said, maintaining eye contact with Martina. Galaxy walked to my left side and sat, looking up at me expectantly. My eyes never left Martina's. "Is it all right if I put the ramp away now?"

"As long as you keep the dog under control while you do it."

I wanted to ask her what Galaxy had done in six seconds of interaction that made Martina think she *wasn't* under control. I wanted to ask her why *her* dog wasn't sitting at a heel on Martina's left side.

More than that, though, I wanted to ask Martina what her problem was. She was there during Galaxy's test. She had seen Galaxy pass. She saw the guy conducting the test actively try to startle Galaxy to ensure she wouldn't snap or freak out and accidentally hurt a patient while working. But I bit my tongue. To do therapy work we needed this woman's approval. Besides, if Galaxy could do what she'd done with the woman in the store, Martina would be forced to recognize that she was born for this. We had to get into the building first without starting a fight in the parking lot.

I put the ramp away, closed the hatch on my car, and then approached her. "All right, we're ready." She took another step back. "The dogs must be kept at least two feet away at all times."

I stepped back as well. "Fine, two feet. That's fair. Are we ready?"

She hesitated. "I heard what you told Tim during her test. Don't think I will be lax because of her past."

"I never expected you to be."

"Some dogs just aren't built for this kind of work."

"I agree."

She was baiting me, which frustrated the hell out of me, but I wasn't going to react. I was determined not to give her the satisfaction.

"The agency is responsible for any injuries that the dog may cause while working. You understand that, right?"

"I do."

"How many backyard-bred pit bulls do you think should be trusted with that responsibility?"

"At least one," I said, flashing her my most charming smile. "Should I wait for you inside?"

Before she could answer, I started walking through the parking lot. Inside I was screaming. Part of me wanted to turn around and drive away. Martina wasn't going to give Galaxy a fair shot, that much was obvious. She would find the slightest misstep and use that for justification to fail us. In her mind, we'd already failed, and nothing was going to convince her otherwise. We were wasting our time. I wanted to run. But I held my head high and strode confidently into the lobby, with Martina close behind me.

"This way," she said curtly, leading me through the lobby and into the volunteer coordinator's office.

"Miss Martina, good to see you," a young man said brightly, standing up from his seat behind the desk. "And Miss Shelby, how are you today?"

Then he saw Galaxy. "And this must be Miss Galaxy! I've heard about you."

I glanced up at Martina. "All good things, I hope?" I asked.

The coordinator crouched in front of Galaxy, reaching out to pet her. "Oh, but she didn't tell me how beautiful you are! Look at that beautiful face!" Galaxy was in her element. She stood up and walked closer to the man, wanting to cuddle with him. Then she sat down again, her butt between his feet and her back to his chest, and raised her head to lick his chin as he petted her.

"Oh, look at you!" he cried. "You're just the sweetest little cuddle bug, aren't you? You're going to have so much fun. Everyone's just going to love you!"

"She's drooling," Martina said.

"Oh, she's just happy," the coordinator told her.

Martina looked at me. "That's not very hygienic. Will she do that a lot?"

"I brought a towel," I answered, pulling out the small hand towel I kept tucked into my back pocket for that exact thing. I knelt, quickly wiped the drool off her face, and then tucked the end back into my pocket.

Chapter Three

Martina scoffed but didn't say anything. After a moment, the coordinator stood up, and Galaxy took her place back at my heel. "All right, I'll check you two in. Here you go." He handed us both stickers that said VOLUNTEER. I placed mine on my shirt. Martina did the same with hers, and then we walked the dogs through the hallway to an elevator. She and Shelby walked in, and she instructed me to stand in the opposite corner with Galaxy.

The doors closed, and the elevator started moving to the second floor. Galaxy didn't expect that and spread her front paws as if she were trying to keep her balance. She let out a soft, startled whine.

"What is she doing?" Martina asked nervously.

"I'm pretty sure she's never been in an elevator before. I think she's a little nervous."

"Nervousness is typically a red flag in therapy dogs."

"And Shelby wasn't nervous the first time she was in an elevator?"

Martina scoffed. "Shelby is a purebred Saluki—a retired show and breeding dog. She was properly socialized from a young age."

"Well, given a choice, I'm sure Galaxy would've preferred such a pampered life, but she just wasn't that lucky."

"I suppose it's not surprising that you consider responsible dog ownership to be 'pampering' dogs."

Well, shit.

Dammit, she'd been baiting me again, and this time I fell for it. I wanted to kick myself. By the time the elevator doors opened, I felt completely defeated. Martina was looking for a reason to fail us, and now she'd found it. This was such a waste of time. There was no way Martina would pass us.

But even though I'd fallen into her trap, I wasn't going to let her fully beat me. If nothing else I was going to show her what Galaxy could do. What she *wanted* to do, if someone would just give her a chance. If Martina could just see what Galaxy could do, that *connection* she could make with people, she'd have to pass her. No one could witness something like that and not be affected by it.

If she could just see *that*, everything would be okay.

We stepped out into the hallway, and I let Martina take the lead. It was easy. All we had to do was let the dogs sit for a few minutes with each patient. None of them had a problem with Galaxy being a pit bull. They all seemed genuinely thrilled to see her, even more so when she'd sit next to them and rest her head on their laps. One woman downright squealed with delight when she stopped petting Galaxy to ask me a question about her, and Galaxy, the impatient Bully that she is, put her nose under the woman's hand and pushed, not-so-subtly urging her to keep petting.

"Oh, she's *delightful!*" she exclaimed, enthusiastically petting her. "What a charming, silly young lady you are!"

A man gave us a wide grin when we walked into his room to find him lying in bed, with a woman I assumed was his wife sitting in a chair beside him. "Oh, I *love* pit bulls! I had so many of them when I was younger. Did I tell you that, Bernice?"

"Not in the last half hour," the woman said dryly from her chair.

The man turned to look at me. "They might look scary, but they're the softest things in the world. They just want to love you, baby. People

Chapter Three

always thought I looked tough when I walked my dogs around, but I'll tell you a secret. The whole reason I liked them in the first place was because I'm an even bigger baby than they are."

"Not a secret," Bernice said.

The man laughed and put his face down to Galaxy. "Don't you listen to that grumpy old woman over there. She doesn't know what she's talking about half the time."

"Says the man not wearing pants."

"Woman, do you see the blanket? I'm decent, dammit. The last thing I want is to offend this delicate lady's sensibilities."

I couldn't help but laugh at their bickering. Bernice looked up and smiled at me, and then turned back to her husband. "Oh, but the *human* women you don't care about."

He scoffed. "They're grown. They've dealt with worse than a frail old man. But this little lady right here, this is a baby. She just needs lovin'."

Finally, Bernice looked up from petting Shelby. "Don't mind him. He's senile."

"Well, you should be grateful, woman. Going senile means I don't remember all your bitching."

"How lucky for me."

I couldn't help but laugh. They seemed to bicker *constantly*, but underneath that, they loved each other.

Suddenly I realized I was enjoying myself. Even with the tension with Martina, I was having *fun*. And Galaxy was just having the best day of her life. All these people were nothing but happy to see her, happy to spoil her with attention, and she was every bit as happy to sit with them and let them pet her. I'd never seen her so relaxed, so comfortable, so in her element.

It was even clearer now that this was what Galaxy was meant to do. Now that she had the chance she was radiant. Her energy was nothing but pure joy, and she was thrilled to be able to share it with every patient.

Chapter Four

Our last stop of the visit was a large room that was some kind of physical therapy facility. Several patients were there, with nurses and aides, doing various exercises on various machines and equipment.

Martina and I made the rounds, but I noticed Galaxy looking over often at one man in particular, sitting in his wheelchair while his aide unsuccessfully tried to convince him to stand up. He ignored her completely, staring off into the distance. He seemed utterly unaware of anything that was happening. His body was slumped over, his hands lying limply in his lap, his shoulders hunched. He just looked so sad, like he'd completely given up on everything and was just waiting to die.

It was hard to look at. But Galaxy kept looking back at him. Every time we left one patient and moved to another, she tried to take a step toward him before moving back to my heel. While she was with each patient, she was entirely focused on them, but whenever we moved, she kept wanting to go to him.

"Come on, Dan," the aide was telling him. "Just stand up for ten seconds, that's all. I'm right here. I'll help you. You just have to try."

He ignored her.

I finished walking around the room, saying hello to all the other patients. Galaxy turned her entire body to face the man, and then looked back at me, almost as if she were asking permission to see him. I glanced at Martina, who was standing with Shelby and another patient. I wasn't sure what the rules were. Were we allowed to interrupt the man's therapy session, especially since it seemed like it wasn't going well? Would the aide be annoyed if we asked to let him see Galaxy? Would she even allow it? Would interrupting the therapy session be breaking the rules?

Then I thought—surely we must be allowed to at least ask if nothing else. Otherwise, Martina wouldn't have brought us here in the first place. I followed Galaxy and stood off to the side.

"Is she allowed to say hi?" I asked the aide.

She turned back to me with a frustrated sigh. "I guess so. He's not going to do his exercises anyway."

With other patients, I'd been guiding Galaxy, showing her where to sit by the patients' side so they could reach her and pet her easily. This time I gave Galaxy the length of her leash and let her take the lead. She walked up to the man as he sat in his wheelchair, his hands in his lap, and licked his fingers. The man blinked as if startled, then looked down at her.

"A *dog*," he murmured, his voice thin and raspy, his words slurred.

Galaxy licked him again, standing in front of him, wagging her tail and her entire body.

"It's a *dog*," he said again and raised one frail, shaking hand to pet her. "I miss my dog."

"Her name is Galaxy," I told him, but he didn't acknowledge me. He seemed not even to hear me. He just kept petting her, staring intently at her.

"I want a dog. I loved my dog."

Galaxy sat in front of him, smiling up at him as if he were her favorite thing in the world. And he just kept petting her, repeating the exact words again and again.

"It's a dog. I miss my dog. I loved my dog. I want a dog."

My heart broke for the man. I wanted to stay with him all day and let him keep petting her. And Galaxy just *adored* him. She seemed giddy, having him giving her attention. All too soon Martina called my name and beckoned for me to leave with her.

"It was nice meeting you," I told the man and started to walk away.

"No, wait! The *dog*!"

"I'm so sorry, we have to go."

"I miss my *dog*!"

Then the aide spoke up. She looked to Martina, who she seemed to know. "Can you stay for another couple of minutes?" she asked. "I might be able to get him to stand up if the dog is here."

Chapter Four

Martina nodded and began another round with her dog and the other patients.

The aide turned to the man. "All right, Dan—you want to pet the dog?"

"The dog," he murmured, still reaching for Galaxy, who was just out of his reach.

"I'll make a deal with you. Stand up for ten seconds, and then you can pet the dog for a little longer."

"I want a dog."

"You want to pet the dog? Then prove it. Stand up. Let's go."

"But the dog!"

"She'll wait for you. She's not going anywhere. But you have to stand up first."

Finally, the man tore his eyes from Galaxy and looked to the aide. There was a moment of hesitation as if he were considering her offer. For a moment, I expected him to simply shut down again and go back to ignoring everything. But then he gave a short, curt nod and held his hands out for her. She took his hands, grabbed him by the arms, and gave him something to hold on to as he rose out of his chair.

His legs were shaking so badly that I was sure he'd fall. After that initial moment, though, he managed to right himself and stood up surprisingly quickly. Once he was standing, he looked back at Galaxy.

"The dog," he murmured, reaching for her.

"You wanna walk to the dog?" the aide asked. "Come on, let's walk to her."

She held him with a hand under his arm to help steady him, while another aide grabbed his wheelchair and pushed it forward, keeping it close behind him. He walked the three or four steps to us, with Galaxy sitting there, watching him get closer and closer, her tail wagging like mad behind her. It felt like she was cheering him on. She kept wiggling her entire body, shifting her weight excitedly from one paw to the other, licking her lips as if he were a juicy steak. In truth, the only time I'd ever seen her do that was when she knew she was about to get fed. She was ecstatic to see this man walking unsteadily toward her. She kept shifting her weight, almost as if she were trying to scoot closer to him, though she stayed at my heel. It took a moment, but finally, he reached her and reached a hand down to pet her.

"That's great, Dan!" the aide exclaimed. "All right, let's sit back down, and you can pet the dog for a minute."

"I love my dog," he murmured, slightly out of breath now. Once the aide had him seated again, Galaxy walked right up to him and plopped her head in his lap, licking his arms and hands with excited enthusiasm. As he continued petting her, she calmed down and sat in front of him, happy to be there with him and share that moment with him.

I see you. I'm here. You're not alone.

"Good dog," he whispered, over and over, so quietly I couldn't even make out what he was saying at first.

"Good dog. That's a good dog."

Martina finished her second round and came up to me. "It's time to go," she said quietly.

I nodded, then turned back to Dan. "We'll be back again," I promised him.

Chapter Four

He looked up at me—the first time he'd acknowledged my existence. "That's a good dog," he said, pointing to her.

I smiled. "Yes, she is."

As we left the room and headed back down the hallway toward the elevator, I felt like I was on Cloud Nine. I didn't even care that Martina was going to fail us. That had felt so *good*. I'd had fun. I'd enjoyed the small talk, the bickering, and the companionship I'd felt with everyone Galaxy spent time with. I was even more convinced that Galaxy was born to do this. She was so happy to be there, to have had the chance to sit with those people. This had been heaven for her. So I didn't care that Martina was going to fail us. There were other therapy dog agencies in town and other testing supervisors. This visit wasn't the end. We'd try again, with someone else.

I couldn't help but be cheerful and hopeful, even when Galaxy hesitated before stepping into the elevator and even though she flinched again when the elevator started moving. We stopped to chat with the volunteer coordinator, and he asked me how our first visit went.

I beamed at him. "It was amazing," I told him. "We had so much fun."

He smiled back at me. "Hopefully it was the first visit of many."

As we left, he gave Martina a wink, and I followed her back to the parking lot. As we went outside, my mood dropped just a little. I was dreading the conversation I knew was about to happen. I couldn't help but play it out in my head, over and over again, trying to come up with something to say, some way to convince Martina to give us another chance. I could spend the next week getting Galaxy used to elevators, escalators, and anything else she wanted. I could make sure Galaxy wouldn't be nervous about them again.

We each put our dogs back in our respective cars. Then I walked to Martina, mentally preparing my defense. Martina went to her front seat and pulled out a clipboard. I waited for a moment while she wrote, but then couldn't hold it in any longer.

"It's my fault," I told her. "I didn't think to socialize Galaxy with an elevator. I can take her out every day and get her used to them. Escalators, people movers, whatever you want I can do. But she loved this. You *have* to see how much she loved this, and how good she was at it. It's not her fault I didn't teach her how to behave in an elevator. I can fix that if you'll just give me a chance."

"Be here next week, same time."

"But she didn't even do anything wrong!" I cried. "All she did was act just *a little* nervous, for less than thirty seconds! You saw how much better she was the second time! Just because you . . . you . . . I'm sorry, what did you say?"

She handed me Galaxy's form. "Bring this with you when you come back. I don't keep them."

"Come back? You're passing us?"

"I'm not passing anyone yet," she corrected sternly. "You still have two more supervised visits left."

She put the cap back on her pen, clipped it to the clipboard, and then turned to face me. "And *you* need to grow a thicker skin."

I was still in shock. "Excuse me?"

"Do you honestly think I'm the only one who will ever tell you that pit bulls can't be therapy dogs? If you can't handle me asking questions, how will you handle a patient, family member, or staff member insulting you? Or being hostile with you? Do you think I will coddle you just because your dog had a rough life? That's not what this is. If you can't handle someone getting in your face, or holding you and your dog to the same standards everyone else is held to, then tell me now so I don't waste my time with you."

I was stunned silent.

She sighed, then relaxed. "I don't know about pit bulls as therapy dogs," she admitted. "But *that* pit bull? She's got a gift for it. I am not easily impressed, but *that* pit bull impressed me. You do that two more times, you've got your certification." With that, she turned and got in her car. I barely managed to eke out a sheepish "thank you" before she closed the door and drove away. It took me a moment to realize I was still holding Galaxy's testing form in my hand. Finally, I recovered from the shock and looked down to read what she wrote.

I was flattered, and I realized then that Martina was right. I couldn't let other people's opinions get to me. There were always going to be people who didn't like my dog or wouldn't like me for having her. Maybe that

was something I could apply to other areas of my life. No matter what I did, there would always be people who wouldn't like me. Maybe they wouldn't like my tattoos, my makeup, my clothes, or how I raise my son. There will always be people who would disapprove of an infinite number of possible things about me.

I could make myself crazy trying to do the impossible and earn the approval of people I didn't care about, or I could turn my focus on myself and the good I could do. Galaxy certainly didn't seem to mind that Martina didn't like her. As deeply in tune with emotions as Galaxy was, there is no doubt in my mind that she knew precisely how Martina felt about her. I'm positive she knew how deeply Martina disliked and distrusted her. But she never took it personally nor let that tension interfere with her. She still had the best day ever, doing something she genuinely loved, and reveling in all the attention she got from the patients. It didn't matter to her that Martina disapproved, and it shouldn't matter to me either.

Maybe I could take a lesson from Galaxy's ability to simply let that kind of tension and disapproval go. Maybe the world didn't have to like me. Maybe I didn't need the approval from everyone I met. Maybe we all could learn to let go of that need for approval and focus on simply living our lives in a way that makes *us* happy. As long as we do our best to make the world just a little bit better, it doesn't have to matter what other people think.

Chapter Five

Our second supervised visit was uneventful, but the third would end up sticking with me. Martina met me at the veteran's hospital, in the parking lot, the same as the other two times.

"Some of these patients aren't going to want to talk to us," she warned. "If that's the case, we just thank them for their time and move on to the next patient. Remember, we're here to make their day a little better. If spending time with a dog won't improve their day, then we move on without judgment."

"I understand."

We walked inside, checked in with the volunteer coordinator, and began our rounds. Just like with the last two visits, Galaxy was in absolute heaven. She loved spending time with people, and all the patients were happy to see her. Some shared their pit bull stories; others just complimented her and gave her love and kisses. She was happy as a clam. But then, we reached one room where the lights were off, with a nurse helping an amputee into his wheelchair.

"Would you like a therapy dog visit?" Martina asked from the doorway.

The man didn't answer. Didn't even look at us.

I thought, *Oh, this must be one of the patients she was talking about.*

You didn't have to be a body language expert to see that he was angry. Even from where I stood in the doorway, I could practically *feel* the rage rolling off of him like he was one heartbeat away from throwing a table at us. I was sure he'd want nothing to do with us. I'd already started moving out, not wanting to intrude or make him feel guilty for saying no.

"What about it, Kev?" the nurse asked. "You want to hang out with a couple of dogs for a minute?"

He hesitated, then muttered, "Fine."
Oh, this is a bad idea.

I followed Martina into the room. Like usual, she stood off to the side with Shelby so I could approach with Galaxy. But I felt nervous. Unsure. This man was missing both legs and fingers from one of his

Chapter Five

hands. He had horrific burns all over his face that seemed to reach below the neckline of his hospital gown.

He'd experienced true horror, unlike anything the average civilian could even imagine. This man had survived a war, leaving him angry, bitter, and closed off. He couldn't have been any older than twenty-five. My heart went out to him, but I was hesitant. I'm not easily intimidated, but the fury rolled off of him in waves, thickening the air in the room. Galaxy, however, was immune to the tension pulsing out from him. She walked right up to him, sat down on the side of his wheelchair, and just plopped her huge head on his thigh.

Plop—no hesitation, no checking to see if he was receptive, and no concern. Just *plop*. And that was it. She didn't move.

She didn't even mind that he wouldn't touch her. With other patients, whenever they stop petting her she'll either shove her nose under their hand or impatiently scoot closer so they'll start petting her again. This time, with Kevin, she seemed content to just sit there, just as still as he was. The only movement she made was occasionally tilting her head just enough to look up at him. It was the most painfully awkward moment of my life. I stood in a corner of the room, hardly breathing, as man and dog stared at each other for what felt like a long time—but was not long at all. I couldn't help but breathe a quiet sigh of relief when Martina called my name.

"Time to move on. Thank you for your time, sir," Martina said. I awkwardly thanked him as well and turned to leave the room. And as soon as I left, I felt so ashamed. He hadn't wanted us there. He'd only done it to make us and the nurse feel better. To accommodate us. I felt so ashamed for intruding on him like that. I felt horrible for it and couldn't escape his room quickly enough. Luckily, the rest of the patients were thrilled to see her, and by the end of the visit, I had completely forgotten about him. I was enjoying myself too much and enjoying seeing how happy Galaxy was. I was all smiles and full of giddiness when Martina handed me the completed test forms, all signed and dated and official.

"Congratulations," she said, smiling for the first time since I'd met her. "You have a wonderful dog. You'll do great." I could barely wait until she left to call Alan with the good news.

"That's amazing!" he said. "We've got to celebrate."

We had dinner at our favorite dog-friendly restaurant in town, where we got to show off her forms.

We'd been there many times before, and most of the wait staff recognized us. "Miss Galaxy!" the waiter greeted cheerfully once we were seated at a table on the dog patio. "Welcome back."

"We're celebrating!" Aaron announced. "She just passed all her tests to be a therapy dog."

The waiter's eyes widened. "That's amazing! Congratulations! What a wonderful thing to celebrate!"

He took our order and hurried away. Within minutes, the manager stopped by. "Did I hear correctly that Galaxy just passed her therapy dog tests?"

I blushed just a little, surprised that the waiter had told the other staff. "Yes, just this afternoon."

"You ordered food for Galaxy, correct?"

"Yes." The restaurant offered a handful of dog-safe meals for their canine patrons, and every time we went, we always made sure Galaxy got some food, too.

"May I please cover the cost of Galaxy's food? May I send out a little after-dinner treat when your meal is finished?"

I was surprised. "Sure. Thank you so much!"

"No, thank *you*," the manager said brightly. She gave Galaxy a warm smile. "You're helping people, and Galaxy is a wonderful dog."

"It was *my* idea to get her," Aaron declared. "She's my little sister."

The manager chuckled. "Well, you had a fantastic idea."

As we ate, all the wait staff came by to congratulate us. While the staff isn't allowed to touch the dogs, that didn't stop them from talking to her and showering her with praise.

When the meal was over, suddenly the manager and a group of waiters walked out, holding a small dog-safe birthday cake on a platter. They all walked over to our table, and the manager turned to address the crowd.

"Ladies and gentlemen, may I have your attention please," she said loudly to the other patrons on the patio. "Please join us in congratulating Galaxy, who just passed her test to become a therapy dog!"

Chapter Five

There were claps and cheers as one waitress set the platter down on the floor in front of Galaxy. Our waiter also held a separate plate with a regular birthday cake, which he set in front of Aaron.

"And this is for being the best big brother in the world," he said. Aaron's face just lit up, completely delighted.

Alan took my hand under the table and grinned at me. "You did a great job," he said quietly. It was a perfect end to a perfect day.

The following day, I sent off the forms and started waiting for them to be processed. I couldn't wait to go back and do more therapy work again. But I knew that processing the forms could take a while, so I was surprised a week later when I got a call, and heard Martina's voice on the line.

"Martina? Is everything okay? Is there something wrong with Galaxy's forms?"

"No, it's fine. I got a call from the veteran's hospital. There's a patient that's requesting you."

"Me? Why me?"

"Well, he's requesting Galaxy."

"Am I allowed to go yet?"

"No, but we'll call it an unofficial supervised visit. As long as I'm there with you, it'll be all right. Are you free tomorrow?"

"Yeah, sure."

"Great. Meet me in the parking lot at 10 a.m. See you then."

"Okay, see you tomorrow."

I hung up and looked at Alan.

"Everything okay?" he asked.

"Yeah. One of the patients requested to see Galaxy this week."

He shrugged. "That's not surprising."

"Isn't it?"

"You showed me pictures of what Martina's dog looks like. Something tells me some veterans might be more comfortable hugging a dog that looks like Galaxy than one that looks like Martina's dog."

"Yeah, but to specifically request her?"

He shrugged again. "I guess you'll have to wait and find out tomorrow."

The following day I was curious as I pulled into the parking lot. As usual, Martina and Shelby were there early, waiting for me.

"Good morning," Martina greeted. "You ready?"

"Sure. So who requested Galaxy?"

"They're not exactly in the habit of giving out patient names over the phone. The volunteer coordinator will tell us which room requested us." I nodded and followed Martina into the coordinator's office.

"Hello!" the coordinator greeted. "You two are right on time. Here are your passes."

She looked at me as she handed me my sticker. "Please make sure you hit Room 218. The patient requested a visit from your dog."

I thanked her, silently wishing I'd paid more attention to the previous week's room numbers. I had no idea who would've requested her. All of the patients were happy to see her. Which of them could have requested another visit? But I put that from my mind as we began our rounds. Martina suggested we do 218 last to ensure we had some extra time to spend. All the other patients would be happy to see the dogs and deserve our attention and focus first.

The visit went well, but as we turned the hallway to head to Room 218, I suddenly remembered where we were and which patient must have requested her. But no, that couldn't be. Kevin had been so angry, so full of rage and bitterness, and we'd forced him to accommodate us when he hadn't wanted us there. No, I had to be misremembering. There was no way he'd been the one to request Galaxy. We walked up to the room to find that, like last week, the lights were off. And sure enough, Kevin sat in his wheelchair, absently watching TV.

"Good morning," Martina greeted him from the doorway. "Would you like a therapy dog visit?"

He glanced over at us, saw Galaxy standing outside the room in the hallway, and then silently beckoned us into the room with a short wave of his good hand. Martina stood beside me, giving me room to go through the door. "I'll get the rest of the patients in this row, then come back and meet you here," she said.

I let Galaxy lead me into the dim room. Just like last week, Kevin didn't speak and didn't acknowledge us at all as we approached him. Also,

like last week, Galaxy sat down next to his chair and plopped her big blocky head on his lap. But then, after a moment, he lifted a single hand and rested it on her head. That was it. He didn't pet her and didn't move; he just stared absently, unthinkingly, at the TV. It felt no less awkward this time, even knowing he wanted us there.

And again, Galaxy didn't mind that he wasn't petting her. She stayed right there, right at his side, her head in his lap, for the whole time. Both of them remained in complete silence. The only sound in the room was the quiet drone of the TV.

I see you. I'm here. You're not alone.

I felt uncomfortable as hell. But whatever comfort he was taking in Galaxy's presence, it was important to him. Important enough that he specifically asked to see her again. Important enough that Martina, who takes this therapy work very seriously, bent the rules to allow us to come to see him. At the end of the day, it wasn't about me. It was about Galaxy and the companionship she can give to the patients. So I accepted the awkward, uncomfortable silence and stayed there, off to the side, just out of his peripheral vision, just as still and quiet as the two of them. When Martina returned and called my name, it startled me. I stepped forward.

"Thank you for your time, sir," I said as Galaxy rose to her feet and started following me out of the room. I'd almost reached the door, where Martina stood waiting when he spoke.

"Same time next week?" he asked.

Unsure, I looked to Martina. My certification wouldn't be processed by then. But Martina nodded, and I turned back to Kev with a smile.

"Wouldn't miss it."

Chapter Six

"Holy crap, that was intense," I confessed as we left the building and headed back out to the parking lot.

Martina nodded. "It can be draining. Especially with veterans."

"Why?"

"Because they've been through hell, and they're constantly surrounded by well-meaning people who expect them to be okay. They have to spend so much of their recovery pretending to be all right to make their friends, family, and staff feel more comfortable around them."

"That sounds . . . lonely."

"It is. And that's why dogs are important. The dogs don't expect them to be okay. They don't have to pretend that they're all right. They can just *be*, and the dogs accept them just as they are." Well, damn. That sounded awful. "Do we have to wait a full week before coming back?"

She hesitated. "Not necessarily, but you probably should. This work may not be *physically* taxing, but it can be extremely mentally and emotionally draining for you and Galaxy. You need to pace yourself if you want to keep doing it long term. That's why we limit all working sessions to no more than an hour. It's easier than you think for one or both of you to get burned out, and then you won't be able to help *anyone*."

I hesitated, considering her words. I had to admit I found some truth in them.

Galaxy loved this work. That much was obvious. She enjoyed helping people. She enjoyed being with people, giving them another soul to connect with. But she always fell asleep on the car ride home and slept extremely well after her visits.

I supposed Martina's words made sense. We both had to pace ourselves, because if it were up to Galaxy she'd just keep going, on and on, from patient to patient, until she collapsed from exhaustion, or until her bad knees gave out from overuse.

"That's a fair point," I admitted, somewhat grudgingly.

Martina chuckled. "It's addicting, isn't it?"

"Just a little."

"Discipline is important. Helping others means helping yourself first. If you burn out, or wear yourself out too much, no one benefits."

"That's true."

She opened her car door. "Same time next week?"

I smiled. "Wouldn't miss it."

The same time next week couldn't come fast enough. I found myself thinking about that veteran, Kev, quite a lot. I wondered how many of his friends and family members came to visit him, forcing their small talk on him, expecting him to participate in their conversations as if nothing was wrong. How often did he have to spend time pretending he was okay? I couldn't even imagine the pain he must have been in, the loneliness he must have felt, to reach out to a stranger and her dog for a connection that didn't require him to pretend he wasn't dying inside.

And who was I to judge him for not pretending to be okay? I felt like a terrible person. What kind of self-centered, clueless idiot expects a severely injured veteran to cater to *her* comfort level?

Thankfully Galaxy was nothing but comfortable with him. Without needing to be told, she knew exactly how to be, how to connect with him, even through the intense fog of his anger and loneliness. I wondered again what it is about her that makes her so good at connecting with people. Was this a product of her trauma?

She was probably one of the few souls alive who could relate, at least a little, to the kind of pain in which Kev was lost. She had endured a hell beyond most people's imagining. For a long time, that pain and that fear had ruled her. We had to teach her how to work through it. She couldn't do it on her own. We had to guide her out of that darkness. Now that she was out, she seemed drawn to people lost in their darkness. With

the woman at the store, the old man at the nursing home, and Kev, she seemed so confident, so sure of herself and what she needed to do.

With most patients, she was expected to sit there and do her silly pit bull grin while everyone spoiled her with attention, which she was always happy to do. Human affection is one of her favorite things in the world. She prefers it to toys, other dogs, playing outside, or anything. Food is the only thing that outranks human attention in her mind, so she is never disappointed to just sit there with her silly pit bull grin while people spoil her with attention.

But people who were wrestling with demons, people who were lost in their pain or fear or anger or loneliness, *those* were the people who most attracted her. As we saw with that old man, those were the people she sought out, even in a crowded room. Maybe she felt like she had a more defined purpose, a more explicit goal. And she did that on her own, without any input from me.

Finally, the day came. I met Martina once again in the parking lot, and once again we saved that room for last. She dropped me off there while she went to see other patients. Again, I was taken aback by the angry energy emanating from him, even when I was standing in the doorway.

"Feel like some company?" I asked.

He nodded, and we walked in.

I assumed it would be the same as the last two weeks. At first, it *was* the same. I gave Galaxy her full leash and let her walk up to him and rest her head on his thigh while I stood off to the side. Again, he put his hand silently on her head.

For a few moments, everything in the room was still, but I refused to allow myself to be uncomfortable. I wasn't there for *my* benefit, after all, but for *his*. This was helping him. Galaxy was helping him. It didn't matter that the silence was awkward to me because it wasn't awkward for either of them. And once I allowed myself to relax I found the silence kind of peaceful. I found myself very *okay* with him not being okay. I was grateful that he'd pushed himself far enough out of his comfort zone to ask for something that helped him, even though I didn't quite understand

Chapter Six

why. It was nice. Just calm, and quiet, and still. I let my mind wander. So when Kev moved it took me by surprise.

It happened suddenly. One moment, he was sitting there, stiff and rigid, full of that anger. In the next, it was as if his entire body just deflated. He leaned far over in his chair, hugging Galaxy. Just *sobbing*. My breath caught in my throat. It happened so fast, so suddenly, I didn't know what to do. For a split second, I was worried that he was falling out of his chair. But Galaxy wasn't surprised at all. The move didn't startle her. She didn't pull away. She just sat there, quiet and steady, as he clung to her and cried openly into her fur. He clung to her so hard the knuckles of the one hand I could see were ghost-white. Galaxy didn't mind. She didn't move, cringe, or even look over at me. Because I wasn't there with them. I didn't exist to them right then. It was just *him*, just *her*, just this amazing, pure connection they made together. She sat there, letting him cry, letting him sob, and letting him scream. She stayed still as he started rocking back and forth as if she were the anchor keeping him from being swept away by the pain he was lost in. She was the rock he could hold on to when he felt like he was losing control.

I see you. I'm here. You're not alone.

Nothing else existed. The room, the people walking down the hallway, the light outside the window, everything else melted away, just like with that woman in the store. Time slowed down, and they created their world where it didn't matter that they were both broken, tortured souls. Where they didn't have to be anything for anyone else—they could just *be*. It was the most heartbreaking thing I'd ever seen.

Both of them had been hurt in ways I couldn't imagine. Both would carry scars with them for the rest of their lives. Both of them had seen the absolute *worst* that humanity has to offer. Galaxy's trauma, pain, and scars gave her the tools she needed to help heal this lonely, suffering man. She was *right there*, in that darkness with him, giving him something real, something *true*, that he could hold on to.

It was such a private, intimate moment that I felt like I was intruding on them just by being in the room. I stayed still, standing to the side, making sure not to make a single sound. I didn't want to risk interrupting this moment that he needed and that Galaxy needed to give him.

Her focus, her strength, and her quiet steadiness were incredible. I found myself truly in awe of it, and of her. I never trained her to do that. I never taught her that. The heeling and the sitting and the staying I taught her, but not *that*. She did that on her own, for no other reason than because that's just who she is.

And this, *this*, was what she was trying to communicate to me with that woman in the store. This was what she wanted to do. This was what she wanted her life, her pain, her trauma, and her healing to *mean*. This was the purpose she'd been trying to show me. I was in absolute awe of her.

Kevin cried for a good long while. Galaxy never moved, never faltered. Somehow I knew, I just *knew*, that no matter how long he cried, no matter how long he needed her, she was going to stay there. She was never going to move, not until he pulled away. Finally, he did pull away. It took him a moment, but he managed to put himself back together and straightened up, wiping his eyes. That's when he noticed me. No doubt he'd forgotten I was even there.

"Sorry," he muttered, embarrassed, the color rising even more in his already-red face.

"For what?" I asked innocently, looking pointedly up at the TV. "Hey man, I'm just hanging out, watching *Golden Girls*. Blanche is an icon—I don't care what anybody says." He gave a soft chuckle and a subtle nod, understanding what I was trying to tell him.

I'm not a therapist. I wasn't there to try and "fix" him or make him pretend he was okay when he wasn't. What he'd just experienced, the emotions that had overwhelmed him undoubtedly made him feel raw and vulnerable. A random stranger wasn't the right person to have seen that from such a reserved man, and I didn't want to make him feel like he had to talk about it or acknowledge it if he didn't want to.

"Thanks," he said quietly. He sniffled and then looked down at Galaxy. "And thank you, you giant ugly tank of a dog."

I gasped with mock outrage. "How dare you! The only descriptors suitable for her are a *stunningly beautiful princess*, thank you."

He laughed. "I'm so sorry, forgive me." He looked back to Galaxy and put his hands on either side of her face, bending over, so his face was a

fraction of an inch away from hers. "Please forgive me, Your Highness. I'm not worthy."

She wagged her tail and licked his face. Without even waiting for him to finish speaking, she just interrupted him with persistent, enthusiastic kisses.

He shot back up, groaning. "Ugh! She licked inside my mouth!"

"Therapy visit with a happy ending. Can't ask for anything more than that."

Suddenly I heard Martina calling me from in the hall. I looked back at him. "We've got to go. See you around."

"Same time next week?"

I turned to grin at him. "I could never stand in the way of puppy love. It's a date."

Outside, Martina stood to the side, out of sight of the doorway, leaning against the wall with Shelby. I got the impression that she'd been standing there for some time.

"Ready?" she asked simply.

"Yeah, let's go."

We waited until we got back outside to talk. I leaned heavily against a big pillar in front of the building.

"Oh, holy shit," I murmured. "Holy . . . fucking . . . shit."

"I saw the tail end of that. How long had it been going on? Since I left you?"

"Not quite," I answered. "But close. How long were we in there?"

"I'm not sure. It doesn't matter, though, does it?"

I sighed, bending down to rest my hands on my knees. "Holy *shit*, man."

"Good job handling it."

I looked up at her, incredulous. "*Handling* it? Look at me! I'm shaking. What *handling*?"

"I heard the *Golden Girls* comment."

"Yeah, Blanche is an icon." I bent back down, trying to catch my breath. Maybe I'd been more overwhelmed than I was willing to acknowledge.

Chapter Six

"That was the right thing to say. Anything else would've just embarrassed him. Making jokes was the right thing to do. It pulled his focus off of the potentially embarrassing thing that had just happened. You ended a draining and emotionally intense visit on a positive note. You did everything perfectly."

"You'd better be careful," I told her, still a little breathless, straightening up and leaning back against the pillar. "Or you're going to make me start liking you."

"Oh, the horror."

"He asked to see us again next week."

"I heard."

"Will my certification be in by then?"

"Probably not. If it isn't, I'll meet you here again, and we'll do the same thing we did today."

"Galaxy isn't the only natural one on your team, you know," she said, giving me the warmest, most genuine smile I'd ever seen from her. "Come on. The session isn't over until the dogs are in the cars and we leave. Go home. I'll see you next week."

In the car, Galaxy fell into a deep and, as always, certainly well-deserved sleep.

As I drove home, I found myself thinking back on Galaxy's first visit with Kevin. Even though I doubted the situation at first, doubted myself, and even doubted *her*, she knew what she needed to do. She never let my doubt stop her from giving Kevin what he needed. She knew something I didn't, and trusted herself, even when I was hesitant and unsure. Galaxy's world was simple. She saw someone hurting and knew how to help.

When we first brought Galaxy home, she was the most anxious, insecure dog I'd ever seen. But in that dark room with Kev, there was no trace of her past insecurity or fear. She had trusted herself with a man who wouldn't even speak to us at first. She had trusted herself and gave an injured veteran a brief reprieve from the bitter loneliness he felt.

Maybe I could take a lesson from her ability to trust herself so implicitly. I thought back on my life to times when I doubted my knowledge and experience because I let the doubt of others influence me. I realized I didn't have to let their doubt impact my choices. I could trust myself the way Galaxy trusted herself with Kev.

Maybe we all could take a lesson from Galaxy's ability to do that. There will always be people doubting us. Sometimes even people who love us and trust us, who have nothing but the best intentions, might doubt us, just as I had doubted Galaxy. But just as Galaxy didn't let that doubt influence her ability to do what she knew she could, we don't have to let the mistrust of others limit us.

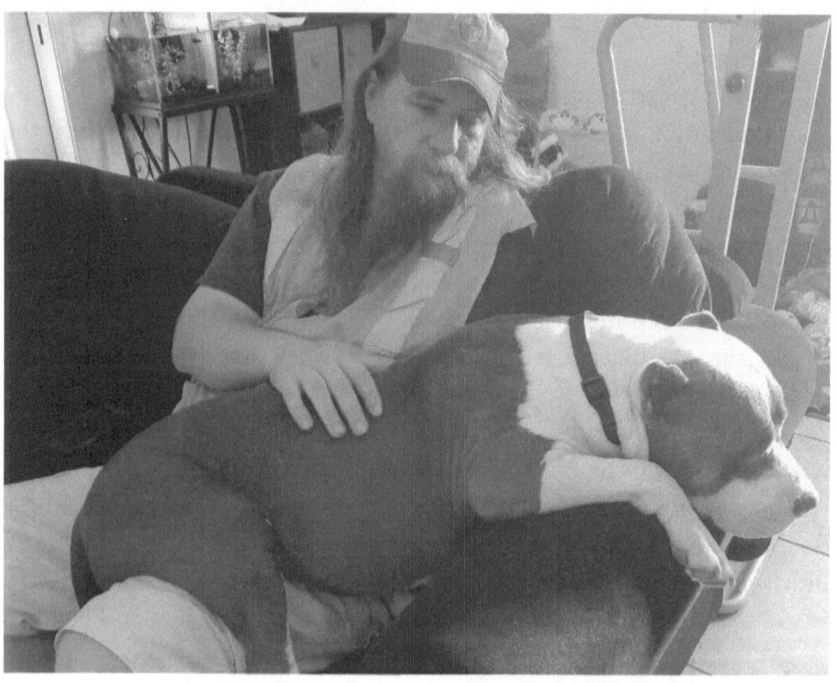

Chapter Seven

ONCE OUR PAPERWORK WENT THROUGH, WE SPLIT OUR TIME BETWEEN the veteran's hospital and the nursing home. Dan, the lonely old man, was still there, excited to see Galaxy. Kev was doing a lot better, too. A few weeks later, he'd gone home to live with his parents but still came for weekly physical therapy appointments.

On one of our visits, he called me over and cheerfully showed me his phone. "Look," he told me, smiling. "Her name is Lexi."

I took the phone from his outstretched hand and looked. On it was a picture of a happy-looking American Bully, black and white, about Galaxy's size.

"Oh, she's beautiful!"

"I just adopted her last week. There are other pictures, too."

I started scrolling through literally dozens of pictures of him and his parents with Lexi. All of them were happy and smiling, including the dog.

"She looks so happy."

"She's such a good dog. Already housetrained, and so outgoing. She just *loves* people. Clingy, though. I almost ran over her a couple of times."

I laughed. "Yeah, that's a common breed trait. I can't tell you how many times I've tripped over Galaxy. They like to be right underfoot."

He laughed. "Or under a wheel, in my case. But Lexi doesn't mind. I was worried that she'd be scared of my chair at first, but it's like she doesn't even notice it."

I imagine that had to feel good for him. He was still learning how to adapt to living in a wheelchair, and I was sure he was *also* having to learn to adapt to the many awkward and uncomfortable reactions to his chair. I

was glad he'd found a companion that didn't notice, didn't care, and didn't see him any differently than when he was able bodied.

"Dogs are too good for this world, aren't they?" I said.

He nodded as I handed his phone back to him.

"My parents are hiring a trainer. I want to teach her how to pull my chair."

"Oh, that's such a good idea! She'll love that. It's great exercise, and the breed is perfectly suited for it. I thought about pulling work with Galaxy, at first. But her back legs just cause her too much pain. She wouldn't have been happy doing it."

He chuckled as he petted her. "No, she's a delicate princess. Aren't you, Your Highness?"

Galaxy wagged her tail and scooted even closer to him, excitedly licking his hand as if to say, "Yes! Yes, I am!"

He nodded and looked back up to me. "See? She agrees."

"You're right. Lexi will love it, though."

"I think she will. She's got *so* much energy! But then, other times she just wants to be a couch potato. I swear she thinks she's a lapdog. I don't have much *lap* to speak of, but she still manages to wiggle her way right on top of me."

"Oh, you'll never be able to train that out of her. Galaxy would be sitting in your lap right now if I let her."

He snuggled Galaxy even closer. "I believe it." Then he straightened back up in his chair, with a happy sigh. "It's going to be great. I haven't had a dog in years. I think she'll be a good friend."

"I have no doubt. There's just something special about them, isn't there?"

He looked down at Galaxy as she sat by his side, her head affectionately in his lap. A smile softened his features, and I realized how handsome he was when his anger wasn't etched into the lines of his face. I also realized how young he was, now that he wasn't scowling. He'd lived through such hell at such a young age, and that hell would stay with him for the rest of his life. Not very many souls will ever be able to understand what that's like, but Galaxy could.

"Yeah, there is. Definitely," he said.

"Lexi will give you a lot of love. You're going to come back, right? I'd love to hear more updates."

"Yeah, they've got me coming back three times a week for a while. I'll keep you updated."

I thanked him, and we continued our rounds.

Everywhere we went, Galaxy attracted a lot of attention. But it surprised me that, in the handful of times we encountered someone who either didn't like dogs or didn't like pit bulls, Galaxy didn't seem to mind at all.

Watching her with those people, I found myself in awe of her *again*. Because she didn't react. She didn't seem to care at all. When someone didn't want her around, she never took it personally. It reminded me of what Martina had told me: not every patient would want to see us.

Galaxy seemed to understand that. Whenever we were at work, she was completely focused, driven, and clear in her goal. She was there to make people's lives better and offer comfort. If her presence wouldn't be comforting to a patient, she never minded it and never took it personally. She didn't even need to be told. She just passed over the person and moved on to the next.

Most people loved her, though. It always made me smile whenever people started talking about their pit bulls, or their friends or family members who owned a pit bull.

I'd had dogs all my life. And whenever I had dogs, I took them out to tons of places with me. But none of my Heelers or German Shepherds or Australian Shepherds ever garnered the kind of attention that Galaxy did.

I loved it. I loved hearing patients' stories about their dogs, whether pit bull or any other breed. I loved being able to share that passion with people. I loved being able to participate in that connection with other dog lovers.

Galaxy loved it, too, of course. Every new patient was her new best friend. She took so much joy from just being with them, spending time with them, and giving them companionship. I couldn't tell which of us loved the work more; her or me.

Chapter Seven

This was what she was meant to do, and she did it beautifully. Every week, when that vest came out, *man*, she was ready. She'd jump up, forgetting all about her arthritis and bad knees, and prance impatiently at the door, staring at me. It felt like she was saying, "Come *on*, woman! I've been waiting here for four whole seconds already! Let's *go*!"

It got to the point that, if anyone said the word *work*, she'd perk up and look at me expectantly, like "Work? Do you mean *our* work? Is it *time* for work? Can we go to work *now*?" She could be in a dead sleep, and it wouldn't matter. She would wake right up.

But work wasn't the only thing we did together. We also had weekly Pit Bulls on Parade outings with our trainer, Tino. It's a class that Tino runs here locally with some of his pittie students. There are usually between five and eight dogs there at a time. We'll go to a park or an outdoor shopping plaza or somewhere else and work with the dogs a bit, wherever there are a lot of people around. There were always some basic training exercises, but mostly it was just a fun outing to get the dogs out and socialize them a bit in a public setting. It was a good experience for

the dogs, and it also helped educate the public about pit bulls, showing those well-behaved dogs in a positive light.

Galaxy always loved it. She made plenty of friends and had some amazing adventures. She even got to ride an escalator for the first time. This was, at first, a terrifying experience for her.

I always found it interesting that as confident and sure of herself as she was when she was working when she was surrounded by pain, fear, or anger, part of her would always be that same fearful, anxious dog that we saw lying in a kennel at the shelter. It was part of the scars she carried with her, I supposed. Part of the pain that would never truly go away.

At one point, I realized that she would always be an abused dog. It was more than just her old injuries and the chronic pain she felt every day—it was part of her psyche. The cruelty she had endured, the pain she had been subjected to, had been woven into her very being. No amount of training or socialization would ever fix that. It would never disappear. The agony she suffered in her early life would continue to haunt her, every single day. She would never have the chance to be a "normal" dog.

I first noticed it when we were out walking at a park in town. A man walked by with his beautiful German Shepherd. I stopped to compliment his dog, and he complimented mine.

Galaxy stayed at a heel, but the German Shepherd wasn't quite as disciplined. He moved into Galaxy's space. His body language wasn't hostile, and he didn't seem like he had any intentions of aggression, but he was certainly an intimidating-looking dog with a dominant personality.

I grew up with German Shepherds. None of that was news to me, and I was fine with the dog wanting to smell Galaxy. Galaxy, however, was less fine. She whined once, and then suddenly snapped at the German Shepherd.

It happened so fast that I didn't even have time to pull her away. Luckily, it didn't seem like she'd been trying to make contact or attack the dog but, instead, had just snapped as a warning, and he immediately understood and jumped back.

I was so embarrassed. I didn't know what to think at first. Galaxy had never been dog reactive. She'd played countless times with her other pit

Chapter Seven

bull buddies, and with lots of dogs of all different breeds and sizes, at the local dog park.

I knew enough about dogs to know that dog reactivity and human aggression are two very different things, two very different processes in a dog's mind, but that was still alarming. What had caused her to react to this dog, now? And would that affect her ability to be a therapy dog?

I got home and called my trainer. Quickly I explained what happened. He seemed to be strangely dismissive of the whole thing, and of her defensive behavior, but agreed to meet me anyway, to see her for himself.

The next day, we met at a dog park but didn't let Galaxy interact with any of the other dogs. He just wanted to see how she was while there were other dogs around. When he saw that she was still every bit as obedient and attentive to me, he became even more dismissive.

He asked me again what happened, and I told him every detail that I could remember. After I related the entire story, he only shrugged.

"Yeah, he got in her space when she didn't want him to."

"But she could've bitten him."

"Maybe. And she could bite if it happens again."

"You seem unnervingly okay with that."

He sighed. "Look. She's been traumatized. She spent the first three years of her life being tortured, and then eking out a shitty existence on the streets. That kind of thing leaves a scar, you know? It turned her into an anxious dog. You're *always* going to have to be careful with other dogs getting in her space before she's ready for it because she's *always* going to want to correct the dog's behavior. How else do you think she can communicate that she's uncomfortable? That's how dogs talk to each other."

"How do I make sure she doesn't accidentally hurt a dog that gets too close?"

"That's part of owning an abused dog. You have to know her triggers and recognize them before they happen. Now you know that a dog with a dominant personality getting in her space makes her uncomfortable."

"Yeah, but if she bites someone or someone's dog, she won't be able to work anymore."

He shrugged again. "Well, that's on you."

"On me?"

"What would you do in her position? She was reactive because she was *scared*. Her fight-or-flight response kicked in. And she's on a leash, so flight isn't an option. What other option does she have? What other action do you think she could take?"

He hesitated, looking down at Galaxy, sitting quietly at my heel.

"She's a good dog, no one could ever deny that. But she's got demons. More than most. She's got a fearful personality, which means she's going to react when something scares her. It's on *you* to keep her safe, and when something happens that makes her feel *unsafe*, it's on *you* to get her out of that situation and make sure she doesn't bite."

I sighed. He was right. I felt so disappointed in myself for not seeing it, for just assuming that she was okay, that she was normal, that she could be a normal dog. I felt like a failure. I felt like I'd failed *her*.

Tino saw the disappointment on my face and gave me a reassuring smile.

"Owning an abused dog isn't easy. Most people can't do it. But you're not like most people. You've got a lot of experience, and you've got the time to devote to her. Think about how terrified she was when you first got her."

I thought back to how completely neurotic and out of control she was. How much of a struggle it was to build her confidence and teach her to trust us. Now she was a completely different dog than the petrified, pathetic little creature we brought home. While she was still anxious around certain dogs, she loved every single person she met.

"Do you think the average owner would've given her the chance to get over that? Or do you think they would've just given up on her?"

"I don't know."

"I do. If almost anyone else had adopted her, she would've either been returned to the shelter, or she would've ended up as a headline. You gave her the chance to be what she is. But part of her, part of what she is, is wrapped up in abuse and pain. She's still scared of the vet, right? Still anxious in new environments?"

"Oh, big time. But nothing like when we first got her."

Chapter Seven

"Exactly. You got her to a point where she can still function, even though she's afraid. But some wounds never heal. Some trauma never fades. You can't fix it. You can't cure it, any more than you can cure the chronic physical pain she's in. All you can do is manage it. That's got to be on you because she's a dog. She'll never be able to manage it on her own."

He hesitated, looking off toward the crowded dog park nearby. "But don't let her run in dog parks anymore. If another dog getting in her space is one of her triggers, you can't control that or manage it in a dog park. All it takes is *one* idiot bringing *one* under-socialized dog to the dog park, and then Galaxy is on the evening news. It's not worth the risk."

I sighed. "I guess you're right."

"But look at her now. She's calm, she's attentive, and she's happy. She feels safe with you holding her leash. She doesn't need to interact with a bunch of other dogs to have a good life, does she?"

"No, she doesn't."

"Exactly. Keep her away from them, and limit her exposure to other dogs."

"But won't that make her more reactive?" I asked. "Sometimes there are other therapy dogs around when she's working."

"They've got to keep two feet of space between them, right? So none of those dogs are going to get in her space. You have nothing to worry about. She's not aggressive; she's not going to suddenly lunge at a strange dog. But she *did* miss out on that crucial puppy socialization, so she's always going to be a little high-strung and anxious. She's just *scared*. Push that fear too far, and she'll react. It's a pattern, and it's predictable. You know what it looks like now, so you can handle it."

He flashed me a charming smile. "And give yourself some credit. You took a dog that was out of her mind with fear and turned her into a calm, stable family pet. That's not nothing."

"I just don't want to make any mistakes with her. She's been through enough."

He made a dismissive gesture with his hand. "Oh, you're *going* to make mistakes. Everyone does. But she knows who you are. She trusts you. And she knows that you're not perfect. I mean, *look* at her. She's a happy, healthy dog, living a good life. That's not going to change because of an occasional innocent mistake. Just protect her, manage her triggers, and you'll be fine."

I felt a little better as I drove home. I realized that Galaxy was never going to be "normal," but that was *okay*. She didn't *need* to be "normal." And I was freaking out, overreacting, over something that wasn't worth freaking out over.

So what if she would never be normal? I didn't need her to be. She was perfect just as she was. I could accept her as she was and help keep her stable when her fear became problematic. I could manage her triggers and keep her out of situations that would only cause her stress.

And if I could accept her the way she is, I could extend that same courtesy to myself. I didn't have to stress myself out over the aspects of my personality or my mental health that were different from how I wanted them to be. I didn't have to be so hard on myself all the time. I didn't have to blame myself whenever I felt like I was falling short.

Galaxy had learned to function, to survive, to *thrive* in a world that wouldn't cater to her special needs. She would never be perfect, but she

CHAPTER SEVEN

still found a way to make the lives of people around her better. She found something she could contribute—a way to make a difference.

We could all use a little of that in our own lives. We don't have to be perfect, with perfect mental health, to make a difference. Some people will always wrestle with demons, but that doesn't detract from their value any more than Galaxy's demons subtracted from hers. We can change the world for the better if we want to, and do it just as we are.

Chapter Eight

I believed what Tino said, but I was still just a little apprehensive when we went to work that week. It was hard to get that experience out of my head. I'd never before seen Galaxy try to bite, or show any kind of aggression. Logically, I understood what Tino told me. I understood why she reacted the way she did, and I knew that she only reacted that way because she was scared of the German Shepherd.

I didn't blame Galaxy for reacting. I blamed myself for making her feel like she had to. I was supposed to be her protector, the one she could turn to when she was scared and uncomfortable, but I hadn't paid attention. She'd been frightened and nervous, and I hadn't seen it. I'd let her down and made her feel like she had to protect *herself* because she couldn't rely on *me* to protect her. She'd snapped because I had failed her.

It was hard to forget. I still felt bad for not recognizing that she was scared, and for not noticing the signs that she was uncomfortable. I felt bad for making her feel like she had to snap to protect herself. It was scary. If she'd made contact, if she'd bitten that German Shepherd, then she would've been labeled as "just another dangerous pit bull." She would've been banned from being able to work. Maybe even put down.

Breed-specific legislation wasn't a big thing where I lived, but it was still on my mind. All it would take is one mistake, one lapse in judgment, one moment of me letting my guard down, and she would end up suffering for it. All it would take is *one* attack by a pit bull like Galaxy, and maybe her entire breed would be banned in the city.

It would've been completely my fault for not recognizing the trigger. That German Shepherd could've been hurt, and Galaxy could've had her life destroyed, all because of my ignorance—because I underestimated just how much her past abuse still affected her. It was hard to let go, but I took a deep breath as I walked through the parking lot of the nursing home, deliberately putting it out of my mind.

That day, she had been scared, but she wasn't scared today. Today she was alert, focused, and eager. Today she had a job to do, and she wanted to do it. We walked in, checked in with the volunteer coordinator, and started our rounds. By now a few of the residents knew us by name and were happy to see us.

It just so happened that there was a class of elementary school kids there that day. They'd come to read to some of the residents. Galaxy loved kids. She loved playing on the floor with Aaron and didn't even mind when Aaron wanted to dress her up. She patiently tolerated all of it, like the kind, gentle soul she was.

Of course, as soon as we walked into the spacious common room every kid gasped and squealed with delight at the sight of a big, happy dog just trotting in. Immediately we were surrounded. Galaxy went around to all of the kids, playfully licking each of their faces and stopping for pets from the teacher and the parent chaperones.

There was no trace of fear, no trace of anxiety, not even a hint of her past abuse and trauma. She was in doggy heaven, her tail constantly wagging as two dozen pairs of little hands petted her all over. We left to finish our rounds, then came back to let the kids say goodbye, and once again she was surrounded by little hands and little faces.

Galaxy was so gentle with all of them, just as gentle as she was with Aaron. She loved them all; she had spent time with them all and even had lain with her head in one boy's lap as he read a story to Galaxy and an elderly gentleman.

The parent chaperones asked for pictures, and Galaxy was happy to pose with the kids, doing her silly pit bull smile for the camera. When we finally left, I felt so much better.

It was silly for me to let myself get so discouraged. Galaxy had a great life. I didn't need to pretend she was perfect, or that she was normal. She didn't *have* to be perfect, or normal, to bring joy to all those people. I didn't have to pretend that she didn't have triggers. I didn't have to worry.

Sure, I made a mistake by not paying enough attention to her when the German Shepherd tried to say hello. I didn't notice the signs that she was uncomfortable, and that was on me, and only me. Now, I knew better. I knew that a dog getting in her space was one of the things that would scare her, and I knew to pay more attention to her, so I wouldn't miss her warning signs when she was nervous.

I had a plan going forward. I would be more cautious around other dogs, and I would make sure to manage situations where other dogs might be present. Now that I knew about this trigger, I could do what was necessary to set her up for success.

I'd made a mistake. Luckily, no one was injured because of my mistake, and now that I knew better I was *okay* with the fact that Galaxy would never be normal. I didn't need her to be normal.

She was brilliant when she was working. She didn't have to be normal to do her job and do it well. Her trauma would always be a part of her, but it didn't *define* her. It was silly to have been so worried about that. I'd been foolish to get that deep in my head and over-think it so dramatically.

Galaxy had already forgotten about it. She was just her regular, happy, cheerful, goofy self, prancing along at my heel, perfectly proud of herself. She wasn't thinking about how I'd let her down earlier that week, or about how scared she'd been. No, she was thinking about how much fun she'd had, how good it had felt to get all that attention from so many people. She was thinking about all the kids who had surrounded her and petted her. She was thinking about their delighted squeals when she'd rolled over onto her back for belly rubs from dozens of eager little hands.

She'd already gotten over the negative experience. This was *my* issue, not hers. I was the one making a mountain out of a molehill. Even so, it was a stern lesson that I could never underestimate her, or how her trauma had affected her. I would always have to be mindful of her triggers. But that thought didn't overwhelm me anymore. This was something manageable. This was something I could do. I could give her structure and set her up for success. I could protect her and keep her safe. I could manage her triggers. I could do this. *We* could do this.

We were going to be all right.

Chapter Nine

"You keep that thing away from me, or I'm going to stab it."

I turned at the sharp, deep voice, and saw a man standing nearby.

We were in Home Depot, on a cool Saturday morning. Our kitchen faucet had started leaking, so I was out shopping for a new faucet. Galaxy was sitting patiently by my side as I looked through the different options.

I hadn't even noticed the man walk up. Not until he'd said *that*.

I looked up at him. He was *huge*, at least six feet two, broad and stocky, wearing a baseball cap and a T-shirt.

"I'm sorry?" I asked. Surely I hadn't heard him correctly. Surely I'd just been startled to have someone talk to me and had misheard him. There was no way he would have said something like that, completely unprovoked.

He glared at me and gestured to the dog. "You keep that thing away from me, or I'm gonna kill it."

I looked down at Galaxy, more confused than anything. She was still sitting there on my left side. She hadn't moved, hadn't growled, and hadn't done a single thing that could be interpreted as threatening.

My heart rate tripled, and I looked around, hoping to see an employee or another customer nearby. The aisle was empty, except for us. Discreetly, I reached for the pepper spray on my keychain and flipped it to the "unlocked" position.

"Why are you talking to me?" I demanded, deliberately raising my voice, hoping to catch someone's attention. I stepped to the side, putting my shopping cart between me, Galaxy, and the hostile man.

"You keep that dog away from me."

"I don't know you. Leave me alone."

Now Galaxy was getting nervous, too. My fear was being transmitted to her, and she stood up, moving to the end of the cart and looking squarely at the man, her hackles raised. He seemed to take that move as a threat, and stepped angrily toward me, stomping his foot. Both Galaxy and I flinched, and I pulled out the pepper spray, aiming it at him.

"Get away from me!" I shouted, hoping the entire store would hear me. "I don't know you! Leave me alone!"

Luckily, an employee, a tall, athletic-looking young man, poked his head around the aisle.

"Hey!" he called, hurrying up to us. "What's going on?"

I turned to him frantically. "Help! He's threatening me!"

"*You're* threatening *me*!" the man bellowed. "You think I won't defend myself?"

He stepped forward again, and now Galaxy lowered her head, and a soft, low growl rumbled through her. Her lips curled in a savage, animalistic snarl, but other than that, she didn't move. She stood there, her entire body rigid, on a razor's edge.

I knew that if the man took another step toward us that would be it. Galaxy would attack him. Not just a defensive snap, like with the German Shepherd. No, this was pure aggression and single-minded determination. I was desperate to get away.

Another employee appeared, having heard the commotion, just in time to see the man take that threatening step toward me. He sprinted down the aisle, and the two employees stood between me and the man, shouting at him and pushing him roughly away.

The man was even more pissed off, having the employees there. He glared at me as they pushed him away. "I guess all bitches need to be kept on a leash, whether you've got two legs or four."

"Shut the fuck up, you asshole," the younger man snapped. The second employee, an older man, kept pushing, escorting the man out of the store, but the younger guy stayed behind.

"Are you all right?" he asked. "What happened?"

"I don't know," I replied, my entire body shaking. "We were just standing here, and he walked up to us. He said to keep her away or he'd stab her."

"Was she growling at him?"

"No! I didn't even know he was there until he said that."

"All right, it's okay. You're okay. They're kicking him out. Don't worry."

A manager walked up and asked what happened. The employee told him, and he looked at me with concern on his face.

"Are you all right? He didn't hurt you? Or the dog?"

"No, he didn't touch us."

He nodded. "All right. Lewis, why don't you help this young lady with her shopping and take her things to her car? Is that acceptable to you, ma'am?"

I took a deep breath, trying to calm my racing heart. I could hear the blood rushing in my ears. "Yeah, thank you."

The manager smiled and walked away, leaving me alone with the young man. "Talk about an eventful day, huh?"

I gave a nervous laugh, still trying to regain my bearings. "Tell me about it."

"Does that happen often?"

"God, no. Thankfully."

"Really?" his eyebrows shot up, and he seemed surprised. His reaction piqued my curiosity.

"Is that surprising?"

He gestured to Galaxy, who was now sitting calmly, though in front of me, rather than on my left side. "She's a protection dog, right?"

"A therapy dog. Kind of the opposite."

"*Really?*"

"Yeah, why?"

"Just the way she reacted. No barking, no lunging, she was totally in control and fearless, and standing between you and the potential threat. Now she's calm again, but standing between you and me. She's keeping you safe because she knows you're upset. Have you ever done protection work with her?"

"No," I answered.

"Not even as a puppy or anything?"

"She's a rescue. I adopted her when she was three. I highly doubt her first owners did anything other than breed her and beat her."

Chapter Nine

"Oh, the poor thing!" he exclaimed, looking down at Galaxy. "Oh, so you know all about assholes, don't you, little girl? Are you okay?"

He crouched down, but still kept his distance, only reaching out a hand, inviting her to come sniff it. Immediately, Galaxy realized this man wasn't a threat, and walked up, sniffing his hand and letting him pet her. "Look at you. You're so pretty, aren't you? Such a pretty face."

Watching him pet Galaxy, and seeing how quickly Galaxy relaxed with him, helped me relax a little more myself. I took a deep, steadying breath.

"You know a lot about dogs?" I asked him. I was surprised at how comfortable he was, cuddling on the floor with a dog that he'd just seen snarling and growling.

"Oh, yeah," he answered, scratching behind her ears. "My folks run a protection dog service. Mostly Germans and Malinois, but a couple of big Molossers, too. Rotties, mastiffs, stuff like that. Have you ever seen the movie *Hooch*?"

"Sure."

"Hooch is a Molosser. A Dogue de Bordeaux. They're big and scary looking. Surprisingly athletic, too."

He ruffled Galaxy's face. "But you're not athletic, are you? You're just a big tank."

Despite the stress I was still feeling, I couldn't help but laugh. "You know you're not the first person to call her that."

He grinned. "What's her name?"

"Galaxy."

"Galaxy? Aww, such a pretty name for such a pretty girl. You scared the pants off that mean scary dickhead, didn't you? Look at this big scary face."

He squished her face, and she wagged her tail even harder, pleased as punch to be getting so much attention from her new best friend in the whole wide world. Already the fear was gone, the altercation with the jerk forgotten.

"Is she spayed?"

"Yeah, the shelter spayed her."

He clicked his tongue. "Too bad. She's got some good genetics and even better instincts. She'd make a great security and protection dog. What's she mixed with?"

"We think she's an American Bully, but honestly she's just a backyard-bred mutt."

He nodded. "American Bullies are great."

"Do your parents work with any of those?"

He laughed. "No, not them. They look intimidating, but they're just not reliably aggressive enough for it. You break into a house with an American Bully, and you're more likely to get licked to death. We do love rescues as pets, but usually they're just not predictable enough for protection work." He paused to squish Galaxy's face again. "But not you, huh? You knew just what to do with that asshole, didn't you? That's right, you were gonna protect the bejeezus out of your mama, weren't you? Such a good girl."

He looked back up at me. "If you ever want to get her some security training, give my parents a call. I'll give you their number. She's got the instincts for it, and you can't train that."

That was twice that he'd mentioned her instincts. I was curious what he meant.

"What instincts does she have?" I asked.

"Untrained dogs usually don't respond to genuine threats like that. Doesn't matter how big and strong they are, they tend to get scared. They'll bark and all that, but when push comes to shove, they'd rather run away. Galaxy didn't do that. She didn't bark or show fear. She also didn't show any out-of-control aggression, which is a big thing. Human-directed reactivity is a bad thing in protection dogs. You never want them to be *reactive*—you want them to be disciplined and in control until the moment comes that they need to act. That's what Galaxy did. She put herself between you and the guy, making herself a barrier to protect you from him. She wasn't lunging at him, but the second he got too close, she would've struck. But then, as soon as the threat was gone and the moment was over, she was calm and balanced again. I could nitpick, sure, but as far as I'm concerned, she did everything right."

He stood up and wiped his hands on his apron. "You're sure she hasn't had any training?"

"I don't know, honestly. But I doubt it. She didn't have a very good life before we got her."

He nodded. "Yeah, people are fucking assholes. But that's amazing. People pay tens of thousands of dollars for a dog that can do what she just did. And she did it completely on her own, without training. And she was a shelter dog. That's impressive, honestly. You've got a really special dog here."

I smiled. "Yeah, I do."

I got home, called Alan at work, and told him what had happened.

"Are you okay?" he asked, his voice sharp with protective worry.

"Yeah, just shaken up a little."

"Maybe some security training wouldn't be a bad idea. Just in case something like that happens again."

"I don't think she needs it," I pointed out. "And I don't think that kind of hostility is likely to happen again."

Alan was less convinced. "I just want to make sure you're not in any danger if it does."

"I have my pepper spray if nothing else. I'll be okay."

And I knew I would be. Usually, when someone didn't like or was afraid of Galaxy, they simply avoided her. Seeing people cross the street or leave the store aisle as we approached was nothing new, and I'd long ago learned not to let it bother me.

This kind of hostility was a one-off, involving a very unbalanced individual. It wasn't the norm, and I'd learned enough about fear in owning Galaxy to know that I wouldn't let myself be ruled by fear the way that man was.

I was fine. We were fine.

Chapter Ten

Life was good. We were happy, Galaxy was happy, we had our work routine, and things were going well. Galaxy still loved her job and still brought smiles and laughter everywhere she went.

But some people, and some patients, were still nervous around her. Some just weren't dog people and wouldn't benefit from a therapy dog visit at all. Others were intimidated by her size or her breed, and we weren't there to make the patients uncomfortable, so we'd simply thank the patient and move on.

Usually, though, we didn't even have to get that far. Galaxy seemed to understand when a person wouldn't benefit from spending time with her, sometimes even before we reached the patient's door. She'd want to keep walking, and after a step or two, as she'd realized I'd stopped, she'd move back to her spot at my heel. She'd wait quietly for me to ask the patient if they'd like a therapy dog visit and thank the patient after they told me no, and she'd move on.

She just had this innate understanding of when she wasn't welcomed, and as I've said before, she'd just move on without taking it personally or getting her feelings hurt. She was good at seeking out and helping the people who wanted to see her, and ignoring the people who didn't. So I was surprised when I got a call from a therapist in town, telling me that the agency had recommended me to him.

"Have you ever considered exposure therapy with Galaxy?" he asked me over the phone.

"I . . . I don't know," I told him honestly. "I don't know what exposure therapy is."

"It's a technique that can benefit some patients with certain phobias," he explained. "Have you ever heard of cynophobia?"

"Yeah, that's a fear of dogs, isn't it?"

"Yes. Sometimes it can be more specific, such as a fear of big dogs, or a specific kind of dog."

"Like a pit bull," I supplied, understanding where he was going with this.

"Exactly. In *some* specific scenarios, it can also help people work through past trauma."

I thought back to the woman in the store, who had been attacked and mauled by a pit bull when she was younger. Her courage to work through her fear and touch Galaxy is what started us on this journey in the first place.

"Galaxy would be fantastic for that," I told him confidently. "That's sort of how we got our start."

"What do you mean?"

I told him the story of that woman in the store, what she had been through, and how Galaxy had made such a beautiful connection with her. He listened quietly until I was done.

"That's exactly what I'm looking for," he said. "Would you be willing to meet up? I have a patient who has expressed an interest in exposure therapy, but if it's all right with you, I'd like to screen Galaxy first, just to see how she is."

"That sounds great."

"And please understand that, if it ends up not being a good match, that in no way is a slight to you or your dog. I'm looking for something very specific to help a young patient work through their fear."

"Oh, I understand completely," I assured him. "We're there to help the patients. If Galaxy can't help a patient, we never take it personally."

"Good," he said, relief in his voice. "When would be a convenient time to meet?"

The next evening, I walked Galaxy into the therapist's empty office, after the last patient had left for the day. The receptionist was still there, and she unlocked the door for us with a big smile.

"Oh, she's beautiful! Look at her. She looks so regal and dignified!"

Chapter Ten

I smiled back, choosing not to tell her that I'd just had to bathe Galaxy that afternoon, after I caught her outside, rolling around in her poop, gleefully kicking dirt and grass up into the air.

So regal. So dignified.

The receptionist walked us back to the office, where a thin, well-dressed gentleman with neatly styled gray hair sat in a big leather armchair. He smiled and rose to his feet to shake my hand.

"Mrs. Wilson, I'm so glad you came to see me. I'm Craig."

I smiled back at him as I shook his hand. "Thank you for calling. We're happy to help."

He looked down at Galaxy as she sat calmly at my heel, looking up at him hopefully. "And this must be Galaxy. I've heard so much about you."

He crouched down to pet her. I noticed him putting his hands on her ears, over her eyes, across her mouth, not to hurt her or cause her discomfort, but to judge how she reacted to being touched in some of her more vulnerable spots. It was very similar to how the testers at the agency had petted her. They'd gone over her whole body, touching her paws, her tail, her ears, everything, to make sure she was comfortable with being touched everywhere.

Galaxy seemed to understand what he was doing. She patiently allowed Craig to touch her, wherever he wanted, and waited until he'd finished his examination. When he was done, he sat back on his heels and looked at her. "What a calm girl you are!"

She stood up, then, taking a couple of steps to him, and then sat back down just in front of him, her back to him, inviting him to pet her even more. When he started scratching her neck and her back, her mouth opened, showing off her charming pit bull grin.

"Does she have a lot of energy?" he asked me.

"Not really. She gets the zoomies sometimes, but prefers the mellow, couch-potato life."

"Is it all right if I try to get her excited? I have a tug rope here. Can she play with that?"

"Sure."

And then I had the absolute privilege to see this well-dressed, deliberate, and dignified man make an utter fool of himself, playing on the floor with Galaxy. He spoke in a high, excited voice, trying to get her to be more excited and playful. Of course, she thought this was just the coolest thing in the entire world. She happily played with him, licking any inch of bare skin she could find, cuddling with him on the floor of his office, and even playing a little bit of tug with him.

After a few minutes, he took a breath and stood up. "All right, that's it," he told her, in a firm, but gentle voice.

She sat down in front of him.

He grinned at me. "I couldn't have designed a dog better suited for this if I'd tried."

I was relieved. "She did good?"

"Beyond my expectations. Even when she plays, she's so mellow, and that's what I was looking for. She doesn't get too intense or excited."

"Well, she *can* get kind of intense when she's afraid. She has some triggers that can set her off."

"Like what?"

"She doesn't like the vet or the boarder. And she doesn't like it if another dog gets in her space."

He waved his hand dismissively. "That won't be a problem. It'll be in a closed conference room, and she'll be the only dog there. Does she react to human fear?"

I thought about the way she'd reacted a couple of months prior, with that man at Home Depot. "The only time she reacted was when a man threatened us, and *I* was scared. But she calmed down right after he was escorted out."

He nodded his understanding. "I think she's a great candidate. I can't tell you much about the patient. We'll call her Laura. She can tell you her real name when you meet her if she wants to. She's a teenage girl who was attacked by a pit bull when she was younger. She's very frightened of pit bulls, particularly big ones like Galaxy, but she's expressed a desire to try exposure therapy."

"What do you need us to do?"

"For the first visit, simply existing in the room is all that's required. I'll show you the conference room. It's larger."

Chapter Ten

He showed us to a big empty room down the hall. "You'll be staying in the far corner, there. Galaxy will need to be sitting, preferably against the wall with you standing sort of in front of her. We'll bring the patient in and let her stay near the door. She's going to be in charge of the session. We're going to take everything at her pace."

"That sounds good."

"Could I show you how I would like you and Galaxy to stand when she walks in?"

"Sure."

I let him guide us to the far corner, and he described how he wanted Galaxy to be. He set her down in the corner, right against the wall, and had me stand in such a way that I would be directly between Galaxy and the girl as she walked through the door. It also served to partially block the girl's view.

"If and when she's ready, she'll ask you to step to the side, but we'll need Galaxy to remain where she is. Can she do that?"

"Not a problem," I said, deliberately stepping to the side to show that Galaxy wouldn't move.

"Good, that's perfect. That may be all she'll be ready for on the first visit, and that's okay. Just being in an enclosed room with a pit bull is going to be a big step for her. We'll need Galaxy to stay just as mellow and calm as she is now."

"That makes sense. If she's excited, even if she's happy or being playful, it'll probably scare the patient."

He nodded. "Exactly. That's the big thing. Lots of pit bulls are very friendly and love people, but they can be playful and energetic. We need one that is specifically low energy and mellow."

"I'll make sure to take her for a walk just before the appointment, to get any excess energy out."

"Good idea. But I think this will be a good fit. My receptionist will give you the appointment date and time. If you're unavailable for that time, we can reschedule with the patient's family."

"Sounds good. Thank you."

We said our goodbyes and stopped by the receptionist on the way out. "Does this work for you?" she asked, handing me an appointment card.

I nodded. "We'll be here."

"Come fifteen minutes early, please. We'll want her already out of the waiting room and in the conference room when the patient arrives."

It was only a few days away, but I was excited. This was something Galaxy had done before. I already knew she was good at it, and knew how to be quiet and soft and gentle with a fearful person. She'd done it before, without needing to be told or trained how to sit or where to stay.

This would be a cakewalk.

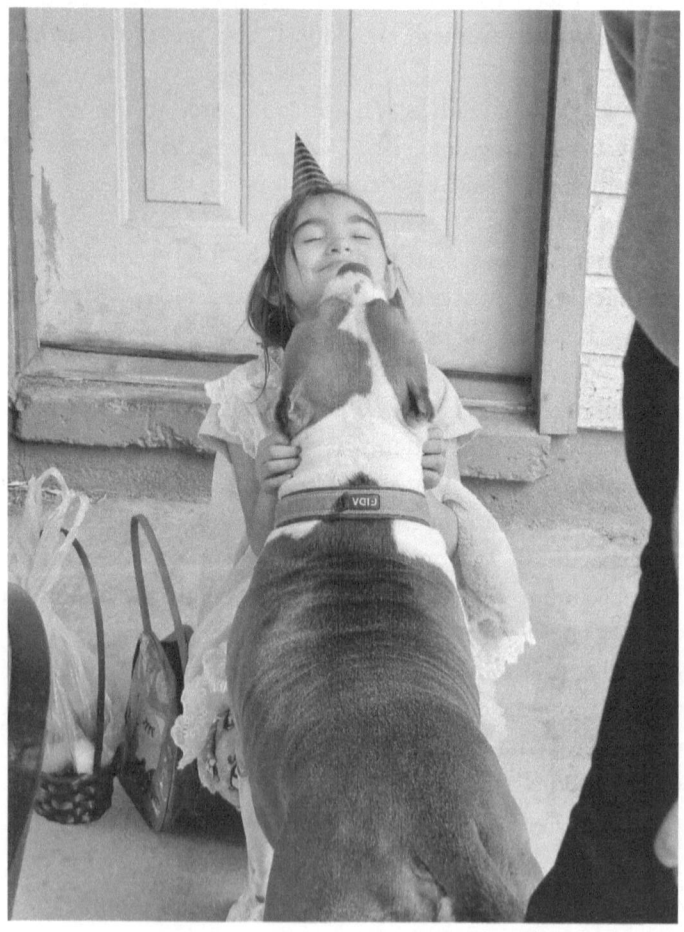

Chapter Eleven

OH, THIS IS A VERY BAD IDEA.

I could feel the tension even before the door opened. It was palpable, and when the door opened and I heard Laura's frightened, frantic voice, I was sure I'd made a mistake. This kind of extreme fear, this kind of tension, this kind of trauma, was going to undoubtedly set off Galaxy's fear and trauma. It wasn't just the girl, it was her parents, too, and they seemed to be even more scared than the girl was.

I could hear them talking in the hallway. The girl was the one who kept saying she wanted to try, she wanted to push through her fear and see the dog. Her high, strained voice was met by lots of gentle reassurance from the therapist.

"You call the shots here," he reminded her. "You don't have to do anything you're not comfortable doing."

"You're sure this pit bull was screened?" Another man's voice. The girl's dad, I assumed.

"Yes, she is an AKC-titled Canine Good Citizen and a registered therapy dog. She is very calm."

"Is she muzzled?" The mother's voice.

"No, but she is leashed and under the handler's complete control. I assure you, you are completely safe."

No, this was too much fear. This was protective anger from the parents and absolute terror from the girl. This was too much, too intense. It was going to set off Galaxy's fear and past trauma.

This, of course, wasn't going to be good for Galaxy, but I also worried about Laura and her family. If they saw Galaxy freaking out, it would only make their fear worse.

This was a bad idea. This was a mistake.

"I want to go in first," the dad said.

"It's all right, I will go in first," Craig replied gently. He addressed Laura. "I'm going to close the door. When you're ready, tell me to open it, and I'll hold it open for you."

"And the dog is leashed?" the mom asked again.

"She is leashed and under her handler's complete control. I'm going to walk in now. Knock when you'd like me to open the door."

"Where is the dog?" Laura asked.

"She's on the opposite side of the room, on a leash, and that's where she'll stay. You'll be able to step out of the room and close the door if you feel uncomfortable. I'll stay between you and the dog the whole time."

I could hear her take a deep, shaky breath. "Okay."

"And you'll make sure the dog stays?" the mom asked.

"Yes, I will."

The door opened, just wide enough for Craig to walk through. He smiled at me and gave me a big thumbs up, then called back through the door. "All right, I'm in the room with the dog, and everything is safe and under control. When you're ready, you can knock and I'll slowly open the door."

I took a deep breath. I was so nervous I was shaking. I wished I could tell Craig to stop, that this was a bad idea. But so far, Galaxy was fine. She didn't seem to mind being told to wait, and she sat there, in her spot against the wall, just relaxing. Just chilling out, as if she weren't about to be stuck in a room with three people who were terrified of her.

We were quiet for a few seconds, but then we heard a faint, timid knock on the door. Craig grabbed the handle and turned.

"Okay, I'm slowly opening the door now," he called. "The dog is quiet, she's calm, and she's under control. You're completely safe."

Slowly, he opened the door, positioning himself so that he was standing directly in the doorway, between the girl and me. Behind him, I could see the frantic parents standing in the hallway, craning their necks to see around him and make sure Galaxy was sitting and that she was leashed.

I could feel their hostility from across the room, but I couldn't blame them. They'd witnessed their daughter being savagely attacked by a pit

Chapter Eleven

bull, and it seemed that they were far less enthusiastic about this exposure therapy than she was. I thought about my young son. I couldn't imagine what they must have felt when their little girl was attacked, and the fear and protective fury they were directing at me now. They were scared for their little girl. My heart broke for them.

Laura, however, seemed to be a little more comfortable.

"She's in there?" she asked quietly.

"Yes, she's over there in the far corner. Would you like me to step aside so you can see her?"

There was a hesitation, then a soft, "Okay."

Craig nodded. "I'm going to step to the side now. The dog and her handler aren't going to move, you're just going to look at them, all right? The second you feel too scared, tell me and I'm going to close the door. Is that okay?"

"Yeah."

"Good. I'm stepping to the side now."

Slowly, he shifted to the side, out of the doorway, and I saw the girl for the first time. She couldn't have been older than fifteen or sixteen. The poor thing was shaking so violently, I could see it even from across the room. Her wide brown eyes were like saucers, her fear pulsing out from her.

She didn't notice me at all, though. Her eyes were glued to Galaxy. Suddenly, she darted out from the doorway, out of sight of us.

"Do you want me to close the door?" the therapist asked. He had already started closing it, but Laura spoke.

"No," she said. "Just . . . I just . . . just give me a minute."

"Take your time. You're completely safe."

I couldn't see what she was doing, but I heard her mother speaking softly to her in the hallway, though I couldn't make out what she was saying.

"No, I *want* to," Laura said. "Just give me a second."

"She's all right," Craig assured the parents. "She's doing great. Just give her some space. This is all going to go at her pace, no one else's. She's in charge here."

Reluctantly, the mother stepped back, and I could see her standing there, watching her daughter worriedly. At one point, she looked up to glare at me, and I was surprised by the seething hate I saw in her face. But no, I let that roll off my shoulders. This was a worried mother who only wanted to protect her daughter. I could relate to that feeling. I wasn't going to fault a woman for wanting to protect her child.

Finally, the girl appeared in the doorway again. This time, she stood still, her eyes glued on Galaxy.

"That's a good job," Craig told her. "What is the dog doing now?"

"Sitting," she answered.

"Very good. How would you describe her right now?"

"Big."

Craig chuckled. "She *is* pretty big, isn't she? But look at what she's doing, and the way she's acting. How do you think you'd describe her mood?"

"I . . . don't know," the girl stammered. "She looks . . . calm, I guess?"

Chapter Eleven

"Good. That's very good. Observation skills are great for helping to break your brain out of getting locked in that fear treadmill. What else do you see?"

Finally, the girl looked up at me. "I see her owner."

"Excellent. How does her owner look?"

"Calm, too."

"Good. Now let's judge our risk here. Now that you see that both the owner and the dog are calm, do you think there's a high risk, medium risk, or low risk?"

"Medium."

"Very good. Do you think you'd like to watch her from the doorway a little more, or would you like to try coming into the room?"

"I want to go in first," the dad interjected. "It's nonnegotiable."

Craig nodded but didn't take his eyes off Laura. "Is that okay with you? Do you want your dad to go in first, or do you want to go in first?"

The dad started to argue, but Craig held up a hand to silence him, still looking pointedly at Laura.

"He can go in first," she said, still staring nervously at Galaxy.

"That's a good idea. Let's have your dad inside."

The man walked into the door and faced me, squaring his shoulders. I didn't need to be a body language expert to understand what he was telling me.

If that dog hurts my daughter, I'm going to kill it.

This was such a bad, bad idea.

But no, the dad didn't matter. The mom didn't matter. We weren't there for them but for Laura. This was all Laura's choice, and no one else's. Laura seemed to be incredibly determined, despite her fear. She *wanted* this to happen. I just had to keep reminding myself of that. Galaxy would know what to do, and how to help Laura. I just had to trust her and trust the therapist, and everything would be okay.

Finally, Laura stepped into the room. But she quickly turned to Craig. "Keep the door open?" she asked.

"Of course, the door is going to stay open." He gave her a big, warm smile. "Look at you! You're in the same room as a pit bull. How do you feel?"

She gave a nervous laugh. "Kinda scared, but okay."

"Just okay? You're doing *great*! Do you still feel safe?"

"I think so."

"Good, just remember, you're in complete control of everything that happens here. If you start to feel uncomfortable, you can walk right out the door."

"I think I'm okay."

The session dragged on, for what seemed like forever. It was beyond draining, but I found myself admiring Laura's determination. To have been mauled by a pit bull must have been terrifying and traumatic. And this girl was completely petrified.

But she had a strength of self and determination that took me by surprise. Even when she was cowering in the corner, trembling in fear, she didn't want to stop or leave the room. Even when her parents kept trying to tell her, "No, that's enough," she wanted to keep pushing herself.

The courage she showed was incredible. It surprised me when, after only about fifteen minutes, she looked at Craig and said, "Can I pet her?"

"Well, we need to ask her owner first. We always check with the owner, first, to make sure it's safe to pet the dog."

The girl looked at me, her fear still very much present in her eyes. "Can I pet her?"

I gave her my most reassuring smile. "She would love that, yes. She's very friendly."

And then, Laura took a few shaky steps toward me.

"Remember," Craig told her, standing by her side. "This is all at your pace. You're in control here."

"But I feel bad. What if the dog gets bored?"

"Don't worry about the dog. This is her job. She's here to help *you*. Even just sitting in the same room is helping you. She knows that, and it makes her happy. She's fine. Her owner is here to make sure she's okay. Your job is to make sure *you're* okay."

It took a full hour, with lots of crying, lots of timidly reaching out a violently shaking hand, only to yank it back and retreat to the other side of the room.

Chapter Eleven

My heart broke for the young girl. She was more frustrated with herself than with anything else. And Craig was fantastic with her, validating everything she was feeling, and helping her work through it.

"I hate this!" she cried angrily at one point. "I keep telling myself not to be scared, and it's not working! Why can't I just *stop*?"

"Think of it like a muscle," Craig told her gently. "This is the first fear workout you've ever done. It's going to be hard, but the more you work at it, the stronger you get, and the easier it will be to do this. But it takes time. Just like when you work out your muscles, if you push yourself too hard, or too fast, it can cause more harm than good. You're doing great. You're already doing better than I expected, and I'm proud of the progress you made. But cut yourself some slack. You can't just go climb a mountain if you've never done it before, right? You have to work up to it. That's all you're doing here. You're practicing a skill."

She sighed, making a conscious effort to let go of the frustration.

"Do you want to take a break?" Craig asked her.

She shook her head, looking at Galaxy with more determination than fear, now. "No. I want to pet her."

"Remember to listen to your body and your mind. We can keep going but don't push yourself too hard. When your body starts telling you it needs a break, you've got to listen to it."

"I'm okay," she assured him. "I want to pet her."

Finally, after a long, emotionally draining hour, Laura was able to pet Galaxy. And then, she let Galaxy lick her hand. Shortly after that, she sat down beside Galaxy and grinned when Galaxy lay next to her, resting her big, blocky head in the girl's lap.

Within minutes, Galaxy was sound asleep, snoring happily as Laura petted her.

"She's very pretty," Laura said to me.

"Yeah, and she knows it, too," I told her with a grin. "She likes using her cuteness to get her way."

"She's growling in her sleep," her mom said, still frightened.

"She's just snoring," Craig told her. "Lots of breeds with that shortened snout snore. But it can sound kind of intimidating at first, can't it?"

"Don't pit bulls just snap, without warning?"

"Any dog can snap when they're startled, but Galaxy is safe. She's got many, many working hours under her belt. Can you imagine the insurance nightmare if they allowed a dog that might randomly snap at people to be a therapy dog? The agencies thoroughly test and screen the dogs before they're allowed to interact with patients."

Chapter Eleven

"During our test, they did their best to scare her and startle her," I added.

"They did?" Laura asked. "That seems mean."

I shrugged. "Maybe, but it makes sense. Imagine if we're sitting with a patient in a hospital. What if a machine falls over or something? They need to know she won't freak out and accidentally hurt someone if she gets scared by a loud noise. They didn't mean any harm by it; it's more a protective measure, because she's so big and strong. They just wanted to make sure she wouldn't hurt anyone, even if it was an accident."

"It goes back to the control we were talking about," Craig told her. "You can't control what might happen in a busy place like a hospital. So you have to focus on what you *can* control. You can monitor and screen the dogs to make sure that they can handle anything that might happen."

"That makes sense," Laura conceded.

"So now, what do you think the risk is, with *this* pit bull? Do you think you're at high risk, medium risk, or low risk?"

She smiled as she looked down at Galaxy. "Low. Very low."

Chapter Twelve

Walking out of the therapist's office, I was exhausted. That was the most intense, emotionally draining experience of my life. And I was so proud of Galaxy. I'd been so hesitant, so sure that the tension and fear and anger in the room would set off Galaxy's fear and her trauma, but she'd done beautifully.

She knew exactly what to do, exactly how to be, to help that girl. There was no hint of her fear, her own ugly and painful past. There was nothing but that pure focus and intent. She was there to do a job, and she wanted to do it well. She'd been perfect. Far beyond the therapist's expectations. Far beyond even my expectations.

Even when Laura was trembling on the other side of the room, Galaxy was reading her and reacting to her, in a way I couldn't, the therapist couldn't, the way no human could. She'd made Laura the absolute center of her world, reaching through the girl's pain and fear, and giving her another soul to connect with.

I'm here. I see you. You're not alone.

It was beautiful to watch.

And of course that was the first visit of many. The kind of fear Laura and her family felt just doesn't disappear overnight. It takes more than one hour with one pit bull to help guide Laura out of that. But it was a wonderful first step. But far too draining to do regularly. Far more intense than Galaxy's regular therapy work. So we didn't do it regularly, maybe only once a month or so. The rest of the time we stuck with our regular patients and our routine.

And Galaxy was happy. But I realized that her ability, her desire to help people, didn't end when the vest came off.

Our in-laws next door had a big cookout for Memorial Day. A bunch of family friends and relatives came over to hang out outside on this beautiful sunny day. Playing in the pool and chatting. Galaxy was having a blast. She kept cycling through to every person, sitting in front of them for as long as they'd pet her. Then, when they stopped, she moved on to the next person. It seemed like her entire goal was just to spend the entire day being petted nonstop.

But then, as evening came and all the kids got out of the pool, I noticed Galaxy paying a lot of attention to an acquaintance's teenage daughter. The girl sat down on the sidewalk, on the edge of the grass, and Galaxy stood in front of her, licking her and being completely fixated and focused on her. It was the same level of focus I saw when she was working.

"That's a beautiful dog," the girl's mom said, walking up to me as I watched them.

I smiled at her. "Yeah, she's a sweetheart. She's taken a liking to your daughter."

"Seems like Shelly's taken a liking to her, too."

Shelly stopped petting Galaxy, but instead of moving on to another person, Galaxy shoved her nose under the girl's arm, trying to get her to keep petting her. The more I watched, the more sure I was. Galaxy wasn't just trying to get unlimited attention. She was working.

I leaned over to the mother. "She's a therapy dog, you know."

"Is she? She seems to have the personality for it."

"Oh, she does. And she's good at it. She tends to seek out people who are hurting."

The woman nodded thoughtfully, looking back to her daughter.

"Is she dealing with anything, by any chance?"

She sighed. "It's been a rough couple of weeks," she confessed. "My ex, her biological father, just passed away. It was very sudden, and took all of us by surprise."

"Oh, I'm so sorry to hear that."

"We weren't close. He was never really a part of her life until recently."

She gestured behind her, to her other daughter and her husband. "You met my husband, Travis, right?"

"Yeah, he introduced himself earlier."

"He's her stepdad, and he's the one who raised her. He's the one she calls 'Dad.' And they're close." She gave another sigh. "But I think she was always holding out just a little hope that she'd be able to have a relationship with her biological father, too. He's gone now, so she just lost that hope. She's feeling sad, but she's also feeling a little guilty, too."

"Guilty? Why?"

"I think she feels like mourning her biological father is disrespectful to her dad. She's worried that being sad over his death will make Travis feel bad, or feel like he isn't as important to her as her father."

"Oh, man, that's a rough position to be in."

She shrugged. "Travis knows what's going on. He assured her, so many times, that he will always love her, and that she's allowed to feel sad because someone she cared about, someone she wanted to love, is no longer with us. But you know how kids are. Big emotions can be overwhelming."

I nodded my understanding. "I think Galaxy can sense that."

At that moment, Shelly leaned over and just hugged Galaxy for a good few minutes. Galaxy didn't move, didn't pull away, didn't budge. She could feel the girl's pain, her loss, her guilt, her loneliness.

I see you. I'm here. You're not alone.

"Yeah, Galaxy can sense it," I said again, more to myself than to the woman.

As I watched them, all of the other people around us disappeared. The sound of laughter and conversation faded away, leaving only a girl and a dog. Nothing else mattered. Nothing else existed. When the girl finally pulled away, her face was a little brighter. Galaxy licked her face playfully, making her laugh. Beside me, her mother gave a soft gasp.

I looked to her, to see her with her hand over her heart, smiling. "She's laughing," the girl's mother told me quietly. "She hasn't done a lot of that lately."

And then, once the girl's mood had lifted, Galaxy turned to look at me, a big smile on her face. She was happy and quite pleased with herself.

It was beautiful. But this wasn't a work day. Galaxy wasn't wearing her vest. This was just a family cookout.

Chapter Twelve

That didn't matter. It didn't matter that there were tons of other people around, or that there were some very enticing smells coming from the grill, or that other kids were running and playing in the grass nearby. All that mattered was that this girl was hurting. That was all Galaxy saw.

I couldn't imagine what that girl must have been feeling. To lose a relative so suddenly, to have that hope for a relationship pulled out from under her, must have been painful. And then, on top of that, to feel *guilty* for mourning the loss of this important man in her life. To feel as if grieving for his loss was disrespecting the man she saw as her dad. To feel as if she couldn't share in that grief with her family without causing them pain. It must have been agonizingly lonely. She was so young. I couldn't imagine how she must have felt.

She hid it well, too. She'd seemed quiet but spent most of the day playing with Aaron and the other kids, swimming and splashing in the pool. I never would have guessed that she was carrying such a heavy burden on those young slender shoulders.

I couldn't see it, but Galaxy could. She could see the girl's pain. She could see her loss, her heartache, her loneliness. She reached right in, through that darkness, to give Shelly another soul to connect with. Someone for whom she didn't feel like she had to push her feelings down to protect. Someone she didn't have to pretend for.

I see you. I'm here. You're not alone.

Again, and it bears repeating, this wasn't something I'd told Galaxy to do. This wasn't something I ever trained her to do. This wasn't even a work day. No, this was just who Galaxy was. Who she wanted to be. What she wanted to give to someone who was hurting.

Galaxy didn't need the vest. She didn't need to be told to sit next to Shelly and let her pet her. She didn't need anyone to point out *this* girl in the crowd. She didn't need any of that. Because it didn't matter to her. She could feel the girl's pain; she could pick her out in a crowded and busy backyard. After a long, full day of socializing and getting spoiled, she found this girl and went right to her. Not because she had to. Not because she'd been told to. Just because of who she was.

I started to fully realize how comfortable Galaxy was with pain, fear, and loneliness. She never shied away from it or tried to avoid it. Quite the

Chapter Twelve

opposite. She seemed to deliberately seek it out. She surrounded herself with it and knew just how to "bully" her way in, past the walls someone had up around themselves. There was never any hesitation, shyness, or feeling unsure. There was none of the fearful nature that we still struggled with in some aspects of her life. In moments like this, with people who were hurting, she was confident and sure of herself, and sure of what she needed to do. She sought those people out. Even when she wasn't working. Even when the promise of food made her mouth water. Even when there were dozens of other people willing to pet her and spoil her with attention.

She didn't want that, though. Not when there was pain she knew she could heal. She sought out those souls who were hurting and gave them another soul to connect with. She gave them a reprieve from their loneliness.

It felt kind of silly, at that moment, to realize that a dog, *my* dog, was my hero, but there was no point denying it anymore. This ability she had, this *thing* she could do, was extraordinary. The fact that she deliberately chose to help people, without guidance, direction, or command, stunned me beyond words. In many ways, she'd experienced true horror; she'd lived through absolute hell and would always carry that pain with her physically and spiritually. But she never focused on it. She never seemed to care. All she wanted was the opportunity to help someone else.

Chapter Thirteen

Galaxy's pain was getting worse. Her back legs were getting worse. It was putting more strain on the rest of her joints, causing arthritis far too early. We were gladly spending a lot on supplements and a specific diet for joint health and improved mobility. That seemed to be keeping her pain at a manageable level. Things were going smoothly. Until one morning. She woke me up at dawn, shoving her wet nose urgently under my hand as I slept. I woke up and looked at her, to see tension in her face.

That's . . . not good.

Immediately alert, I sat up.

She whined softly and walked to the doorway of the bedroom, then turned back to me, as if she wanted me to follow her. I was worried. She'd never done anything like this before. So I followed her out into the living room, to the front door.

As soon as the door was cracked, she barreled outside, only to stop at the edge of the grass. For a moment, she stayed still, her head lowered.

And then she started heaving. She threw up—nothing but brown liquid and bile.

Once she was finished, I brought her back in to let her get some water. That's when I noticed another brown puddle in the corner by her bed. She'd already thrown up, at least once. After she finished drinking, she went back outside. I walked her back out and saw her furiously eating grass, trying to settle her stomach.

I cleaned up her mess inside and looked everywhere I could around her bed, trying to find something that might give me a clue as to why her stomach was hurting her so badly. Her toys were all intact, she hadn't gotten into the trash, and there was nothing that gave any indication that she'd eaten something she wasn't supposed to.

Alan walked out just as I was finishing cleaning up. He'd been awakened by the commotion. He hesitated when he saw me cleaning up the mess, and Galaxy lying on the tile, panting with discomfort.

"What's going on?" he asked.

"I don't know. Galaxy woke me up. She's sick."

He looked at his phone. It was still early, and a weekend, so our regular vet was closed. "Do you think you should take her to the vet?"

"Well, she just had water. Let's see if she'll eat a little bit of breakfast first. If she can't keep that down, I'll call the emergency vet."

"Want me to feed her?"

"Yeah, please. I'm almost done here. Only give her about half her normal breakfast."

He called to Galaxy, and she eagerly followed him into the kitchen, waiting by her bowl to be fed. She ate it all, without hesitation.

I finished cleaning up and walked in to see Alan watching her greedily wolf down her food. "That's a good sign," I told him.

"Yeah, we'll see how she handles it."

We waited a few minutes, and sure enough, she started heaving again. I ran to let her outside, and she threw up all the food and grass, and even the water that she'd consumed since waking up.

Alan stood behind me as I watched her.

"I think it's time to call the vet."

"I think you're right."

I helped Galaxy into the back of my SUV, and we drove her to the emergency vet. Throughout the entire drive, I kept looking back to check on her, but she wasn't heaving anymore. She just lay in the back, panting.

I was worried. This wasn't like her.

Normally she loved car rides. Car rides meant she was going to work, or the park, or hiking, or the pet store. They usually meant good things were happening, and she was always excited. Not this time, though. This time, she lay down in the back, panting, only occasionally moving to try and relieve some of the discomfort she felt.

I pulled up to the emergency vet and got her out of the car.

Now, along with being in obvious discomfort, she was anxious and scared. She'd gotten much better about the vet, no more screaming or trying to hide under my chair. But underneath her goofiness and friendliness, she was still a timid, fearful dog, and the vet was still terrifying to her. She clung to me, practically bumping into me with every step as I walked her into the lobby.

We got checked in and sat down to wait. Now Galaxy started whining, just like she used to when we first brought her home. But being able to sit closer to me and lean against me seemed to comfort her.

A few minutes later we were brought back to an exam room, where a vet tech asked what was wrong. She took notes of everything I said, then told us the vet would be in soon.

Luckily we didn't have to wait long before the vet walked in. We went through every detail I could remember about that morning and the previous night, trying to pin down what Galaxy might have eaten, and what might be wrong.

"Let me take her back for an X-ray and to get her vitals."

He took the leash and started to lead Galaxy out. But she was scared, and in a lot of pain and discomfort, so she pulled back. Finally, I had to walk with him to the doorway, so she'd follow him the rest of the way.

"Poor thing," Alan murmured once we were alone. "She's not having a good day."

"Yeah. I hope it's nothing serious."

He took my hand and gave me a reassuring squeeze, then stood up to look out the window. Just at that moment, a door down the hall opened, and none other than Galaxy tried darting out. Two male vet techs were on their hands and knees, trying to keep hold of her.

"Oh, shit," he said.

"What is it?"

"I don't think she's making friends and influencing people."

"What?" I asked, incredulous. I stood up and looked, just in time to see them wrangle her back in the room. "What happened?"

"That guy opened the door and she tried to run out. She barreled right into him. I think she knocked his drink out of his hand."

Chapter Thirteen

I sighed. "Oh, good. So it's going well," I joked to try to lighten the mood.

A few minutes later, a sweaty vet tech brought her back into the room. Although she knew *exactly* how to heel and walk on a loose leash, she was pulling him with all her weight, and he had to lean back to try and keep control of her.

The first thing I noticed as she cowered by my side was the smell. Galaxy smelled like rotten fish and coffee.

"I should tell you, one of the guys accidentally spilled some of his coffee on her. It wasn't hot, don't worry, but I thought you should know."

Alan laughed. "Yeah, I saw part of that. Looks like you guys had quite the adventure."

"We tried to take her temperature. She, uh, disagreed."

"She didn't try to bite or anything, did she?" I asked. As terrified as she was, trembling near me, I wouldn't have been surprised.

"Worse," he answered. "She expelled her anal glands and tried to bolt out the door. That's what the rotten smell is. Took three of us to wrestle her back in. We managed to get a decent X-ray, but we weren't able to get a temperature."

"You can do it now," I suggested. "She'll listen to me."

He gave me an apprehensive look as if he didn't quite believe me. "You sure?"

"Yeah, she's always calmer when I'm here."

He hesitated for a moment, then shrugged. "All right, let's do it. Give me a second. Let me grab the thermometer."

I ended up having to hold her hips to keep her from sitting down, but Galaxy remained still and allowed the tech to get her temperature. He chuckled as he straightened up to record the reading. "There were three of us on the floor, trying to wrestle that dog," he said with a grin. "You barely have to hold her, and she's fine."

I laughed. "She's a mama's girl. Dad's her buddy, but when Mom says to knock off the bullshit, she knocks off the bullshit."

"Yeah, I can see that. I'm going to put her temp in her file. The doctor will be in shortly to discuss the X-rays."

"Thank you."

Once the door closed, Alan knelt in front of Galaxy to pet her. "You reek, dog," he said affectionately. "Look at this terrible vicious mutt. You made that poor man drop his coffee."

"Making friends and influencing people," I repeated dryly.

The vet walked in a few minutes later and sat down. "Well, we didn't see anything conclusive in her X-rays," he told us. "But that doesn't always mean there's nothing there. Lots of things that don't show up on an X-ray can still make a dog sick. And she seems a little bloated."

"What should we do?" I asked.

"Well, you can take her home and see if the nausea passes. The fact that she can't hold water down concerns me, but we're also looking at her stress level. She's a very different dog when you're around."

"Yeah, the tech told us about her adventures," Alan said with a laugh.

The vet nodded. "I'm concerned she might have an obstruction. We can keep her overnight to watch her, and see if she can hold down food and water. Hopefully whatever's in her system will pass on its own."

He sat back. "But the other thing that concerns me is her anxiety. Keeping her here is probably safer, but because she's so stressed out, it also means that it's less likely she'll be able to pass anything on her own. It might be more expensive for you down the line."

"If she has an obstruction, how serious is it?"

"Deadly," he answered honestly. "And it can get really bad, really fast. If it's a partial obstruction, she's far more likely to be able to pass it if she's at home with you, where she can relax. But if it gets worse, you'll need to bring her back right away. On the other hand, if we keep her, her stress will all but guarantee that she won't be able to pass it on her own."

I looked at Alan, unsure. What was the right decision? Do we prioritize her emotional health at the risk of her getting worse? Or do we let the vet keep her, where they can watch her and act immediately, even though it'll be one of the worst nights of her life?

Which was the right call? What should we do?

"What would you do if it was your dog?" I asked the vet.

He sighed. "There's no easy answer," he admitted. "Either way, it's a gamble. I don't know your financial situation."

Chapter Thirteen

"We've got good pet insurance," Alan put in. "We're not worried about the cost."

The vet nodded. "If money is no object, I'd recommend keeping her. It might be slightly worse in the long run, but bloat can kill a dog within hours. They'll be fine when you go to sleep, and by the time you wake up in the morning, it's too late. I'd recommend keeping her here."

"Then do it."

She cried and pulled her hardest when the tech came to take her back to the kennel where she'd be spending the night. Her scared cries tore my heart to shreds. I wished there was a way to tell her that we weren't abandoning her, that she'd be safe there, with the doctors who could help her. I wished there was a way to assure her that she would be all right.

All she wanted was to come back home with us. I wanted that, too. I ached to be able to save her from this terrifying and uncomfortable situation. But as much as it killed me, I had to prioritize her life over her mental and emotional health. If she had an obstruction that turned into bloat it would kill her. I just couldn't feel comfortable taking that risk.

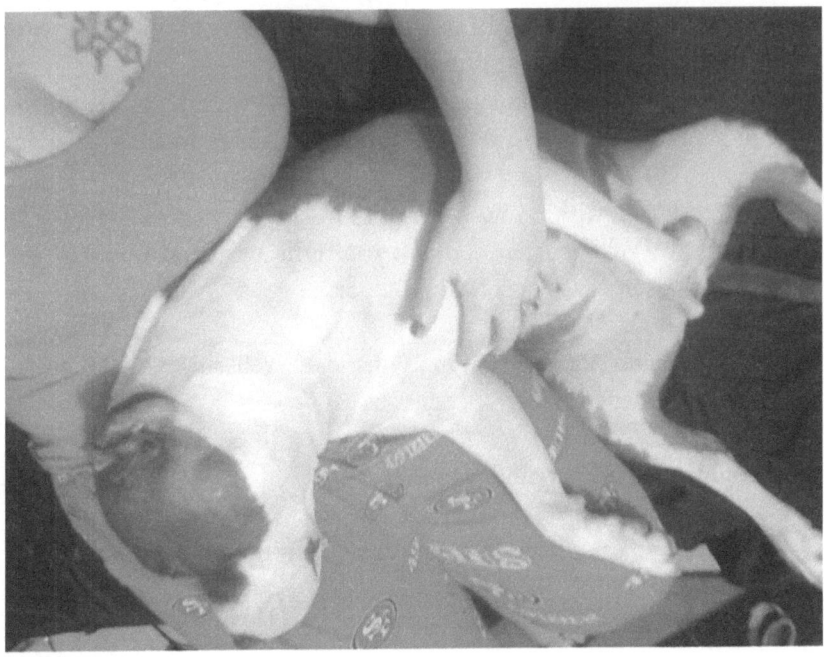

I *had* to let them take her, and I knew they'd take good care of her. She was in good hands, far more knowledgeable and capable than ours. This was where she needed to be—no matter how much it scared her, and no matter how much it hurt me.

I was feeling pretty low as we drove home, and Alan kept reaching for my hand. "We did the right thing," he told me. "We made the right call."

"I know," I whispered. "It just doesn't feel any better knowing that."

He sighed. "Yeah," he agreed simply.

The night was stressful. Galaxy threw up again when they tried to feed her dinner. They gave her IV fluids to manage her dehydration and told me they'd call again in the morning with an update after she'd had her breakfast.

I was up early, staring at my phone, willing it to ring. Finally, it did.

"We fed Galaxy this morning. She ate about half of the food and threw it up almost immediately. She hasn't shown an interest in food since then."

Oh, that's not good. "That's big," I told her. "She's very food motivated."

"I see. We're still not seeing any progress and nothing on the X-rays. Have you considered the possibility of surgery?"

"I think we have to, at this point, don't we?"

"Our surgeon will be in later this morning, so we can get her scheduled right away. We'll email you a quote, but you're looking at about $8,000."

"Do it," I said, without hesitation.

"All right. We'll get that quote to you right away, and we'll call you as soon as the surgery is over, with an update."

"Thank you."

I hung up and put my head in my hands. "Well, shit."

"What happened?" Alan asked.

"She needs surgery."

I could see the worry in his eyes.

"How's she doing?"

"She tried to eat a little of her breakfast, but then threw up, and now she won't eat at all."

His body stiffened. "That's a bad sign."

Chapter Thirteen

Food was the only thing that outranked human affection in Galaxy's mind. For her to refuse food was a big problem. It hit me just then, how serious this was. We could legitimately lose our dog.

But no, I couldn't let myself think like that. The vet knew what she was talking about. The surgeon knew what they were doing. No matter what was wrong they'd be able to find it and fix it. Galaxy would be okay, and this would be nothing more than a bad memory.

But that didn't make the hours of waiting any easier. We tried watching funny movies to take our minds off of what was happening but ended up zoning out more often than not. We were scared of what might happen—what news the next call might bring.

Finally, later that afternoon, the surgeon called.

"She made it through surgery, and she's recovering now," she told us.

"Oh, thank God. What was the obstruction?"

"That's the thing, we didn't find anything," the surgeon said. "We went through her entire intestine, and there weren't any blockages. Some redness and swelling indicative of irritation, but judging by her symptoms, that's not very surprising."

"So there was *nothing*?" I asked, incredulous. "What made her so sick?"

"We think the swelling caused her initial discomfort, and then the stress exacerbated it. But she's fine now. We're going to keep her until she eats and has a bowel movement, and then you can come take her home."

"Okay, thank you."

I hung up the phone and turned to Alan. "There was nothing there," I said, my voice tight with frustration. "Just irritation and some minor swelling. We should've just brought her home. We put her through all that stress, pain, and exploratory surgery for *nothing*."

"Not for nothing," he told me. "She was sick. We had no way of knowing what caused it. We erred on the side of caution, and now we know she's okay." He moved to sit next to me on the couch and put a comforting arm around me. "We did the right thing."

I sighed, leaning into him. "Nothing about this feels good. None of it feels like we did the right thing."

"Of course not. We're worried. She's scared and doesn't understand what's going on. Nothing about this was a fun experience for anyone. But now we know she's okay. That she'll be okay."

Galaxy was finally able to keep water down later that evening, and then a small amount of softened bland food. When she ate her breakfast the next morning and had a bowel movement, we were ready to take her home. The vet techs gave us instructions on what to feed her and how to take care of her until she could get her staples removed, but we were just thrilled to see her.

Her incision was massive. They certainly weren't kidding when they said they had to open her up. The incision was longer than my forearm.

I felt bad for putting her through that, but honestly, I was just relieved to have her home, and on the path to recovery.

She was certainly happy to be back home with us, even though she was moving much more slowly. She seemed to forgive us for abandoning her at what I'm sure she interpreted as the place of indescribable torture and, once home, wanted nothing more than to cuddle endlessly with us. I was eager to give her all the cuddles she could stand. Hopefully, we'd never have to deal with something that scary again.

Chapter Fourteen

When the pandemic hit, it was scary. Living in Las Vegas, a big touristy town, we were very aware of how many travelers and tourists we have, all the time. Most of our state's income is based on tourism, so losing all those tourists was going to hurt. Further, Alan worked for a gaming company. So when he got the call that he was being laid off, no one was all that surprised.

But luckily, we had a bit of a nest egg. My mother had recently died and left me with some money to help see us through. A lot of people were hurting and struggling. I was just grateful that we were okay. And I had to admit, it was nice having Alan at home during the day. Aaron's school went online only, and we all became homebodies. It was the greatest months of Galaxy's life. Lots of walks, lots of love and attention, lots of movie nights cuddled up in our laps on the couch.

I found myself a little jealous of her. She had no idea how scary the world was becoming, how stressful it was to have Alan laid off, and how carefully we had to budget our money to get us through.

The world was falling apart, and she was the happiest she'd ever been.

She didn't even mind that she couldn't go to work during the shutdown. I think she still missed it, but she loved having the whole family there, all the time. I found myself wishing I could be as happy as she was. But she was intent on bringing us all joy and a brief reprieve from the stress of the world around us. We played and had picnics in the backyard; we went for walks in the neighborhood. It was great. And I just felt so grateful for my life and everything I had. I knew a lot of people were struggling.

Galaxy's favorite spot to sit during school hours was in the kitchen. Aaron always sat at the kitchen table for his class, and Galaxy was always on the floor, right next to him. Quietly watching, almost supervising Aaron's Zoom classes with his teacher. She even got some camera time during a show-and-tell session, where all the students had the chance to show off their pets. And of course, Galaxy always had to "help" us with the cleaning and household chores. Somehow, she became even more of a Velcro dog, constantly attached to someone's hip.

More than once I got up off the couch to go into the kitchen and grab a drink, and she'd get off the couch as well, to follow me. She'd happily trot after me into the kitchen and would always find a way to stand in the most inconvenient spots.

"You're standing in front of the fridge," I told her, only slightly exasperated, for the third time that day. She wagged her tail and grinned up at me, leaning against the refrigerator door.

"I'm serious; you're in the way. You need to move."

Chapter Fourteen

I gently pulled open the door, trying to encourage her to get out of the way. She begrudgingly scooted an eighth of an inch to the side.

"Yes, thank you. That's very helpful. A little more, please."

I slowly pulled the door open a little wider, and she moved another inch or two. It was enough that I could reach in and grab my drink. "You know, I don't need your help."

She replied by wiggling her entire butt and moving to lean against my legs, wanting to be petted. I couldn't resist. She was just too cute. All she wanted was constant love and attention, every waking moment, for the entirety of her life. A simple dog, with simple desires.

And I couldn't help but spoil her a little bit. In a frightening pandemic, where we didn't know what the future would hold, she was one of the few things that could consistently keep us from spiraling into fear and dismay. As we struggled to deal with the symptoms of depression in an eight-year-old boy who was now isolated and forced to endure something we didn't know how to help him handle, Galaxy was the stabilizing influence in our family.

And I was frustrated. I didn't know how to help Aaron. I didn't know what to do. No one did, because no one had ever experienced anything like this before. All my research and reading online was far less than helpful. I suggested he start journaling, but his depression made him apathetic and uncaring. He couldn't be bothered to do it, even when I bought him a nice journal of his own.

Galaxy seemed to understand that Aaron was struggling and spent a lot of time with him. Not playing, often not even interacting. Just offering that quiet, calm companionship. She wanted to give Aaron another soul to connect with when he felt alone and lost. More than once, I'd open the door to his room to check on him and find him lying on the floor, watching videos on his phone, with Galaxy lying right beside him. I was grateful that Galaxy felt such a need to be there, with Aaron, but I hoped this shutdown would end soon. I was scared for my son. I was worried about his mental health and felt so helpless and unable to do anything for him.

We contacted some of his friends from school and got their phone numbers, so Aaron could call and FaceTime with his friends. That seemed to help a bit. But it was still a struggle. I don't know what I would've done without Galaxy there, to be Aaron's companion when he was feeling low and lonely.

Eventually, things slowly started opening up again. We were grateful for the ability to wear masks to protect ourselves, and Aaron was happy to be able to go hiking and to the park again. All of us were. We made sure to wear masks and keep our distance from others, but we were just happy to be out in public again. It was strange, how much we'd missed that. Galaxy loved it, too. We ended up, all three of us, going to the park one weekend. Aaron had gotten Alan into playing Pokémon Go with him, so they wanted to go catch Pokémon in the park and asked if I wanted to go with them.

"Sure. I'll let Galaxy run around in the dog park for a bit if it's not too busy."

Ever since Galaxy's run-in with the dominant German Shepherd, I'd made a habit of avoiding dog parks. Tino was right; it was too easy for problems to happen, too easy for an under-socialized or aggressive dog to cause an issue, and I didn't want to put Galaxy in a position where she felt she needed to defend or protect herself. But as long as she was feeling good, and there was only one or two other dogs in the dog park, I felt comfortable letting her get a little of her energy out. We pulled up to the parking lot, and there was only one other dog in the dog park. Oh, perfect, this was exactly what I'd been hoping for.

I turned off the car. "Okay, you two have fun. I'll be here unless it gets too crowded."

"Sounds good," Alan said. He turned in his seat to look back at Aaron. "Ready, kiddo?"

"Yeah!" he exclaimed happily, already opening his door.

They went off to catch their Pokémon, while I opened the back to get Galaxy. She was excited, prancing impatiently as she waited for me to pull out her ramp and clip her leash to her collar. She dashed down the ramp and tried to head straight for the fence, where the other dog was already waiting to meet her. I hesitated for a moment, just watching the dog as he stood at the gate. I wanted to make sure he wasn't too high energy, wasn't going to try and get into Galaxy's space, and wouldn't get

Chapter Fourteen

frantic or make her frantic. But he appeared to be a polite, well-socialized boy, calmly watching us at the gate, alert and tail wagging, but calm. Yes, this would be fine. "Hold on a second," I told her. "I've got to put this away first."

She waited as patiently as she could manage as I folded up her ramp and tossed it back into the back seat. After I closed up the car and locked it, she eagerly headed to the gate.

"Good morning!" I greeted the other woman there, who owned the black Lab prancing at the gate, excited to meet us.

"Good morning," she said brightly. "That's a beautiful dog."

"Thanks, she's a sweetheart."

I opened the gate and barely had the chance to unclip Galaxy's leash before she darted off, running side by side with the black Lab, instantly wanting to play.

I laughed. "They made friends fast," I said to the woman.

"Bruno's a ladies' man. He always makes friends with all the girls."

I chuckled, watching Galaxy play with Bruno. After their initial run together, they finally stopped to sniff each other and sort of introduce themselves. Then, after that quick introduction, they went right back to playing. It always amazed me, just how easy it is for dogs to make friends. All they wanted to do was play. And Galaxy was having the time of her life. She'd sleep very well once we got her home. As she and Bruno continued to play, however, I noticed her starting to favor her back left leg. It wasn't overtly noticeable, but she was just a little slower to start running; when Bruno would suddenly change direction and dart the other way, it took her a second to catch up with him.

I sighed. She was only six years old. Far too young to have to deal with this kind of pain. Far too young to have it affect her like this. But then, as I watched her, I noticed that it didn't seem to be upsetting her. She still wanted to play, run, and wrestle with Bruno. Whatever pain she felt ranked far lower on her list of priorities than her new friend did. And Bruno didn't seem to mind that she couldn't quite keep up with him, either. He was young, healthy, and agile, and would dart a few yards away, then play bow and wait for her to catch up.

"Is she limping?" Bruno's owner asked me.

I sighed. "Yeah, she does that a lot."

"Is she okay?"

"Yeah, she's got bad knees. The people who owned her before us were pretty cruel to her, and that's one of her old injuries."

"Old injuries? What happened?"

I described to her the rough shape Galaxy had been in when we got her, and all the damage that had been done to her. The woman gasped, absolutely appalled. "That's unthinkable!" she exclaimed. "How could anyone be so cruel? To break her legs like that? Why would they have done something so awful?"

I shrugged. "I wish I knew. The only thing I can think is that maybe they didn't want her anymore, so they abandoned her and broke her legs to keep her from following them back home. But we don't even know how long ago it happened, so that's just speculation. I honestly can't imagine what reasoning they had, if any."

"Well, I'm so glad that she found you. She looks very happy."

I grinned. "Oh, she is. And we're just as lucky, honestly. She's a great dog. And she doesn't let her pain stop her from having fun. Bruno doesn't seem to mind, either."

She scoffed. "Oh, Bruno's an idiot," she said, casting a quick, affectionate glance at him. "Good thing he's so cute because there's not a thought behind those eyes."

I laughed. "He's a Lab, right?"

"Yeah. They're supposed to be retrieving dogs. Athletic and intelligent and all that. But not Bruno."

I couldn't help but chuckle. "Well, the two of them are a perfect match. Between the two of them, they have one good body and one good brain. It's a match made in heaven."

We let the dogs play for a good few minutes, and then, when Galaxy's limp started to get a little more pronounced, I called her back to take a break and sit with me for a few minutes.

"Can I pet her?" the woman asked.

"Sure, she's very friendly."

The woman called her name, and Galaxy happily trotted over to sit literally on the woman's feet and get petted.

Chapter Fourteen

"Oh, look at you! You have such a giant head! No wonder you're a smart cookie!" She looked up at me. "My goodness, her head is almost bigger than mine!"

"Yeah, she's a big baby."

"Pit bulls are so misunderstood, honestly. I love them, but I could never own one. How do you deal with all the prejudice?"

I shrugged. "There's more good than bad out there. I guess it bothered me at first. But we've had her for a few years now, and it just doesn't bother me anymore."

"Well, I've never met a pit I didn't like, but sometimes, if people bring pit bulls here, you'll see some people take their dogs and leave. Some will say some nasty things, too."

"Oh, yeah, I've heard some of those kinds of comments. The last time we had to take her to the vet was to get her staples removed from abdominal surgery, and a woman wouldn't even sit in the lobby with us there. She told the front desk staff, very loudly, that she didn't want to be in the same room as a dangerous dog."

"What? That's terrible! What happened?"

I laughed. "The front desk staff all love Galaxy. We take her there once a month to monitor her weight. So they know her. They told the woman, 'That's fine, we'll bump them to the front of the line and get them in an exam room right now, so you won't have to wait in the lobby with them.'"

The woman laughed. "Good! At least, if you have to deal with that prejudice, something good comes out of it."

"That's usually the way it is. Some people are scared of her, and some get downright hostile; but most people love her."

"Well, of course they do! Look at this loveable face!"

After a few minutes of rest, Galaxy was still favoring her back leg, so I decided it would be best for me to leave. I waved goodbye to the woman, gave Bruno some goodbye pets, and went off to find Alan and Aaron. Galaxy was still happy and in a fantastic mood, practically prancing along at my heel. She'd had so much fun. Maybe, as long as her limp wasn't too bad, I thought I might start bringing her to the park a little more often.

She was still nervous and anxious around particularly assertive or aggressive dogs, but as long as the park was mostly empty, it would be a great chance for her to get out and make a doggy friend or two.

Chapter Fifteen

"Is she still limping?" Alan asked the next morning.

"Yeah, a little bit."

"Do you think it's worth taking her to the vet?"

I hesitated. "I'm not sure. She can still put a little weight on it."

"Maybe it's worth calling them anyway."

I looked down at Galaxy as she lay on the couch, her head in my lap. The vet still caused her so much anxiety and fear that I hesitated to take her unless it was necessary. But, given Galaxy's history, and the old injuries we still had to manage, maybe Alan was right. I picked up the phone, called the vet's office, and explained what happened.

"It might be a good idea to have her seen," the receptionist told me. "I can set an appointment for you early next week. Limit her activity until the vet can examine her. Don't let her jump up on furniture, don't let her use stairs, and keep her leashed when you take her out to relieve herself."

"Is it that serious?"

"It's impossible to say," he pointed out. "Pit bull types tend to have a high pain tolerance, which can be an issue when you're trying to judge the severity of injuries or illnesses. But generally, if a pit bull is in enough pain to have a noticeable limp, it's a sign that the dog should be checked out."

"Oh." That was a really good point.

Galaxy was in constant chronic pain; we knew that much. But she rarely showed any outward signals of the pain she dealt with. For her to be hurting badly enough to limp probably wasn't a good sign. I hung up the phone and told Alan what the receptionist said.

"Keep her off the furniture?" he asked. He gestured to her as she snuggled with me on the couch. "How are we going to keep her off the couch?"

He was right. The couch was Galaxy's favorite spot in the house, even more so than her bed. It was her comfort spot. It felt unfair and wrong to deprive her of that when she was already in pain.

"Maybe we can get her a step stool or ramp or something. Just something to limit the impact, so she's not having to jump up onto the couch."

He nodded. "Take a look and see what's available. We don't want to risk making anything worse."

So that day I headed out to Petco alone. Normally I take Galaxy with me when I go there, and this time I felt a twinge of loneliness. That's when it hit me: Galaxy was always going to be in pain. I knew that. I had accepted that long ago, but she never let it bother her or stop her. She never dwelled on it, so I wouldn't either. We'd do whatever was necessary to monitor her pain and give her the best life possible. But now this felt different. Not only did she have to stay home when I went to the pet store, but she couldn't even work that week.

Chapter Fifteen

It wasn't just that she was in pain—it was the fact that her pain was only going to get worse. It was going to age her far too early and eventually would require some pretty significant treatment to give her even a shadow of a fulfilling life. Eventually, she would have to retire from a job she truly loved and wanted to keep doing. And that hurt, way more than I expected.

I found myself feeling irritable and angry as I walked into the pet store. Galaxy was a *good dog* that had been tortured and beaten by cruel, sadistic people. Nothing I did, nothing we did, nothing *anyone* could do was ever going to change that.

She was still so young! She still had so much life ahead of her, still had so much joy she wanted to bring into the world. This was all she wanted, and she was going to end up being cheated because of the abuse she had endured. I was angry. I found a dog steps set and left the store as quickly as I could.

When I got home, Galaxy was still lying on the couch, stretched out and taking up the entire thing, with her head resting on the armrest. She looked up at me as I walked in, and she started wagging her tail. Despite my foul mood, I couldn't help but smile at the familiar *thump* of her tail hitting the couch.

Alan stood up to help me unbox the thing. Now Galaxy's curiosity got the best of her. She slid off the couch and limped over to us, trying to examine the new thing I'd brought home.

"Geez, nosey, much?" Alan asked playfully as she wedged her way in between us, wanting to get a closer look at the new steps.

But Galaxy didn't seem to mind that she was constantly in our way. She stayed right next to us as we read the instructions and quickly assembled the steps. It was a little annoying having to work around her, but even so, we couldn't help but laugh. She looked like a shift supervisor, carefully monitoring our work.

The assembly instructions were pretty simple, and we had the steps assembled and ready to try out within a few minutes. Alan pushed it closer to Galaxy, so she could inspect the finished product.

"Does it meet your standards?" he asked her.

She looked up at him, her mouth open and tongue hanging out in that silly pit bull grin of hers, wagging not just her tail, but her entire body.

"I think she approves," I said.

"Well, let's give it a try."

He stood up and carried it over to the couch.

I hurried into the kitchen to grab the bag of dog treats. As soon as she heard the bag, Galaxy trotted happily into the kitchen after me. She had no idea what was going on, but she was excited about it.

I pulled out a treat and used it to lead her to the little steps. Now she seemed to realize what I wanted, and her eagerness ebbed a bit, replaced by fear and uncertainty.

Watching us figure out how to put it together was one thing. She saw it just as a fun new toy. But something she had to use? A new thing she had to trust enough to walk on? That was a different story.

She tried to move away and lie on her pet bed.

"Yeah, that's a vicious dog, right there," Alan said dryly.

I knelt, holding out a treat for Galaxy. It took some coaxing, but I finally convinced her to get back up and walk over to me. She gave the steps an uncertain sniff.

Finally, after a good few minutes and tons of positive reinforcement, she managed to put both front legs on the bottom step.

"Yes!" I cried, giving her the treat and showering her with love and praise. "Good girl! That's such a good girl!"

It's no exaggeration when I say it took more than twenty minutes to finally convince her to use the steps. Once she did, she stood on the couch, smiling proudly, her tail wagging.

Alan stood beside the couch, petting her. "Yeah, you showed those terrifying steps who's boss, didn't you?"

Galaxy leaned heavily into him as he petted her, very pleased with all this attention she was getting. After a moment, she lay down and curled up in her spot.

He straightened up.

"We'll have to stay on her, and make sure she doesn't try to jump up without the steps."

"I think that once she gets over her fear of it that'll be easy. Whenever I take her anywhere in the car she always waits for me to set up her ramp to walk down. She was scared of that too, at first. Remember?"

As it turns out, it wasn't that difficult. Galaxy was still hesitant, sure, and kept trying to sneak around to the side and jump up onto the couch without using it. But the more she used it the more comfortable she became.

It was one of Alan's favorite things to joke about. Galaxy *looks* intimidating. She's big, she's stocky and solid, she's got the chopped-off ears, and she's got a giant head with obviously powerful jaws. There's no doubt that she could do a lot of damage if she wanted.

Chapter Fifteen

But no, she was always more scared than anything else. The fear she'd been raised with had woven itself into her psyche, her very being.

At the vet, as we waited for her appointment to come up, I made sure to watch Galaxy to keep her from running or jumping. Instead of letting her run around in the backyard I always took her out on a leash. Thankfully she knows the command, "Go potty," so that made things easier. She kept wanting to explore, but it didn't seem to take her long to understand that she wasn't going to be allowed to do that anymore, and adapted.

It always amazed me, this ability she had to adapt to anything. I was angry at the pain she was in, angry at the people who caused it, but Galaxy never acted like she cared. She never whined, pouted, or threw a tantrum. She simply accepted that this was how life had to be, and she still found things to take pleasure in.

It was the same with her pain. She was never angry or defensive; she just accepted that it existed and found things that still gave her joy. Even when the pain slowed her down, she was still happy to be with us—happy to cuddle on the couch, happy to live the spoiled, pampered pet life.

Maybe I could take a lesson from her ability to just let things go. There are and will always be parts of my life I wish I could change. There were always going to be things I wish were different. Instead of mourning what I can't do, or focusing on what I can't change, I could still find happiness and even joy in the parts of my life I *do* love. I could focus on my husband and son. I could focus on my friends and the hobbies I enjoyed. I could focus on small, happy, peaceful moments with my dog, cuddling with her on the couch.

I could find a way to adapt to the things I couldn't change, just like she could, and still find happiness in my life, just as she did.

Chapter Sixteen

Her limp was better, but still noticeable, when the day came to take her to the vet. As much as I hated to think it, I was relieved that she was still limping. I wanted the vet to be able to see how she was moving and see the pain she was in. Our vet was awesome, there was no question, but it's always easier to examine an animal when the symptoms are still present and noticeable. So I was relieved, but it also worried me. It had been almost a week since she'd hurt her leg. If it was still hurting her now, did that mean that she had a serious injury and was just downplaying the pain? Had we reached a point where she was going to need surgery on her bad knees?

Finally, the vet walked in, with a vet tech following close behind her.

"Good morning," she greeted me. Then she turned to Galaxy. "Hi, Galaxy! How are you today?"

Galaxy, the same dog that had screamed at this same woman all those years ago, at our first vet visit, now walked eagerly to her, wanting attention.

"Oh, yeah, I can see that she's limping," the vet told me, her eyes scanning Galaxy's body as she petted her giant head. "Her posture looks good. Let me check her spine and her hips. Sometimes spinal pain can cause limping, too."

Galaxy stood there, her tail wagging, while the vet tech distracted her by talking to her and giving her treats. Meanwhile, the vet ran her hands all along Galaxy's spine, down from her neck to her hips.

"Her spine and her hips feel good. I'm just going to check her range of motion."

One by one, she picked up each of Galaxy's back legs and slowly stretched them as far back as they would go, one hand on each knee joint.

"There's some thickness here, a little bit of resistance. It's worse in her right leg than her left."

"It's worse in the one she's *not* limping on?"

"A little bit, yeah." She stood up. "We'll do some X-rays, but nothing feels broken, so that's a good sign. If we were looking at a dislocation, she wouldn't be putting any weight on it at all."

They coaxed Galaxy to follow them out of the room, to the back. I didn't have long to wait. The tech brought Galaxy back only a few minutes later, with a promise that the vet would be in soon. Galaxy came right to me and sat down between my legs and the wall, leaning heavily against me. Her entire body was trembling.

A few minutes later the vet walked back in. "Well, her hips and spine look pretty good," she said, flicking the light so she could show me the X-rays. "There's no hip dysplasia. That's a good sign. And I'm not seeing anything in her spine that would be causing her pain."

"Here's her left knee. It's arthritic, but not extremely so. Here are the healed fractures, right here."

She sighed. "What's happening, I think, is that the misalignment of her back legs has changed her gait. It's putting an extra strain on *all* her joints because she's had to change the way she moves."

"The other vet told us she'd eventually need surgery."

"She might, but I honestly don't think it's going to help her."

"Why not?"

"Because that's not the primary problem today. The problem is that she's got arthritis in all her joints, particularly her knees and elbows. That's exacerbating all of the pain she's feeling, and it's making everything worse. The arthritis is the bigger issue, because of that added strain due to her gait."

"So we're too late?" I asked, worried.

"It's not about being *too late*," she said. "The surgery wouldn't have helped her to begin with, and the pain she feels is mild and easily managed. It's only now with her arthritis getting worse that she's showing signs of being in pain."

"But her arthritis is made worse by the old injuries?"

"The misalignment caused her to change her gait, which is making the arthritis worse, yes. But her bones were already long healed by the time you adopted her. We don't know for sure how old she was when her legs were broken. The gait was already established. Surgery wouldn't have changed that, and we'd still be in this same position, even if you'd done it right away."

I sighed. At least this time I was able to avoid putting Galaxy through an expensive, painful, and unnecessary surgery that wouldn't help her. But the prognosis sounded grim.

"So what's causing her pain now? Is it the arthritis?"

"No, the arthritis isn't that bad. I think it's a strain or a sprain. The issue with arthritis is that it can interfere with the healing process, so it's taking her longer than usual to heal. Just keep her activity to a minimum for the next two weeks. I'll give you some meds for pain. She's still relatively young, and we're catching it relatively early, so I think we can get her on a good management plan that will help her a lot."

"That sounds good. Thank you."

I checked out at the front desk and loaded Galaxy back into my car. As I drove home, I didn't know whether to be more relieved or sadder. On the one hand, she didn't have any serious injuries and needed only rest. We had medicine and a plan to help manage her pain. We managed to avoid the surgery we were bracing to eventually need. But on the other hand, it now meant that her joints were taking on more damage than they should. And there was nothing I could do about it. No treatment, no surgery, no magic wand I could wave to fix the strain on her joints. I was going to have to watch her lose her mobility and far sooner than was fair.

Now the realization that she was eventually going to have to retire from being a therapy dog felt so much more real. She was going to lose doing this thing she loved. It hit home that we had a time limit. There was a very distinct and very real end to Galaxy's ability to do it.

I was upset. But Galaxy, the pure, simple soul that she is, sat in the back seat, looking out the window, just enjoying the breeze as we drove, smiling at passersby and people in the cars next to us. There was none of the dread that I was feeling. None of the fear that had gripped her at the

Chapter Sixteen

vet. She was happy, just enjoying life. I decided to stop by our favorite coffee shop, Dutch Bros, to get her a cup of whipped cream.

The woman who took our order squealed with delight when we pulled up, with Galaxy's head hanging out the window.

The woman found her entirely endearing and grinned when I asked for the cup of whipped cream. "A tasty snack for a pretty lady."

As we pulled up to the window, a young man leaned out of the window to see Galaxy more clearly. "Oh, man, that's a beautiful dog!" he exclaimed. He called another one of his coworkers, wanting him to see Galaxy.

Galaxy was excited as could be to be getting all that attention, even though the employees couldn't touch her because of the health code. Galaxy didn't seem to mind that they couldn't touch her. She just loved having them talk to her and coo over her.

The young man handed me my drink and Galaxy's cup, then flashed her one final smile before we pulled away. I found a spot and parked the car, then turned back to hold out the cup for Galaxy. She eagerly stepped up to push her entire big nose into the cup, gleefully licking every drop of whipped cream out of it.

Watching her helped calm my nerves. In her mind, there was no reason to dread the future. At that moment, she didn't care that her pain was getting worse. She wasn't thinking about the fact that she was going to have to retire from her job. She didn't even care that she had to take the next two weeks off work. All she cared about, all that mattered to her in that moment, was that she got to eat a tasty treat and she'd been cooed over by the employees at the coffee shop. Even with the pain she was in, that made her happy.

The unfortunate truth was that pain was nothing new to her. Even with us working to manage it, she was no stranger to pain. It was a daily part of her life. But to her, it wasn't important enough to interfere with her ability to enjoy life. She still took joy in all the things she loved, like whipped cream and new friends. The future didn't matter to her. Even the fear she'd felt at the vet's office didn't matter to her. All that mattered was how much fun she was having *now*. Watching her was such a great reminder that I didn't have to let my worry about the future interfere with my ability to enjoy *today*.

Whatever the future brought, whatever fate had in store for us, it didn't matter. We still had today, that moment, offering a cup of whipped cream to a dog that was honestly just happy to be alive. I admired Galaxy's ability to let go of a scary morning and just have fun. It amazed me that, even years into owning her, she was still teaching me so much about letting go of the things I couldn't control.

I couldn't control her pain. I couldn't control the arthritis that was quickly becoming a problem. I couldn't control any of that. But what I *could* control was how I would feel now, in that moment, just spending some quiet time with my dog. I could let go of my fears and worries about the future. The future was going to happen soon enough. There was no escaping it. But it didn't have to loom over me like a dark storm cloud. No matter what happened, no matter how bad Galaxy's mobility got, we would still have moments like this, her and us, together. Just taking quiet happiness in being with each other.

No matter what else happens, these moments will always be ours, and they will always be enough.

Chapter Seventeen

Dogs are such emotionally complex creatures. Their entire worlds are ruled by emotion. Even the way they communicate with each other is based on body language and emotional energy. Every part of how they perceive and process the world around them is filtered through emotion.

It's always been amazing to me how well they can read the emotions of other dogs, as well as people. It's even more amazing when you remember that human ways of expressing emotion are different than theirs. A different "language," of sorts.

Smiling is just one easy example. Facial tension and baring teeth are very clear signs of aggression in dogs. But we speak a different "language," and with us smiling means friendliness and happiness. This is something dogs aren't *born* knowing. Smiling is an inherently aggressive gesture for them. They don't innately understand that a smiling human is a happy human. It's something they have to *learn*.

The fact that dogs can learn what smiling means to us is extraordinary. It is amazing to me that they can genuinely understand that what *they* interpret as an inherently aggressive gesture is something positive to us. There's so much about our ways of expressing emotion that is foreign and alien to dogs, but they can learn so much about us that they get to a point where they may understand us even better than we understand ourselves and each other. Not only do they learn our emotional expression as a second "language," but they can speak it *better* than we can. And they choose to use that ability to help us and give us companionship.

Galaxy is not the only dog with the ability she has. There are stories of other dogs with this gift, and this desire to help people. There are stories of other dogs that have this incredible ability to seek out people who are in pain and need help, wiggle their way through the walls and defenses a person has put up around them, and settle in around their heart.

Galaxy is the first dog *I've* ever known with this ability, this gift, but again she's not the only dog that has it. So many people tend to underestimate what all dogs can do, and how well they can understand us. Their ability to learn our language is nothing short of extraordinary.

As I've said here many times, Galaxy's appearance often gave people the wrong impression about her. Some people would see her size and breed and feel intimidated or afraid. Fortunately, while the prejudice was still there, most people tended to love her. She attracted a lot of attention wherever we went. I still got tons of compliments on how beautiful, well behaved, and polite she was.

During our weekly Pit Bulls on Parade outings, the dogs always attracted a lot of attention and got a lot of compliments. Whenever someone would show an interest in petting her, Galaxy always had a blast. Luckily our trainer, Tino, was incredibly patient and always willing to stop to let people pet the dogs. He always said that his goal was to change the way pit bulls are perceived and that a great way to do that was to let people see them for themselves. He always encouraged people with an interest to come up and pet the dogs, ask questions, or just spend time with multiple well-behaved pit bulls.

And Galaxy certainly loved it. She was always calm, always happy. She couldn't always physically keep up with the other dogs when they jumped on benches and such, but she enjoyed every moment of being the center of attention.

People always seemed so happy to see the dogs, and Galaxy was always happy to let them pet her. Most people just found it a joy to be around her.

But there were less-than-positive things, too. People who pulled their kids closer, or crossed the street while we were walking. People who refused to wait in the vet lobby with us. I had grown men too scared to pass me packages over our fence because she was in the yard—UPS, FedEx, and pizza deliverymen that she would have licked to death!

Chapter Seventeen

On the whole, though, these reactions were easy enough for me to ignore. And it never bothered Galaxy in the slightest. Especially the couple of times it happened while she was working. She could feel that the person didn't want her around—that her presence wasn't going to be beneficial to them—and she simply moved on.

Her focus, when she was working, was to move to the people she *could* help. The people who wanted her there. When she wasn't working,

she also never cared. Her focus was on the people who liked her, the people who approached me to compliment her, trying to see if she could convince them to pet her for every waking moment of her life. So I was getting better at letting those negative reactions roll off. They didn't affect me or Galaxy. There was no reason to react to them or let them get to me.

Though sometimes that was easier said than done.

I'd had Galaxy for years. She'd been nothing but the sweetest girl. She'd worked hard to overcome her fears and learn to find happiness in a world that hated her. She'd done nothing wrong. Nothing to warrant the kind of hostility and fear that was sometimes directed at her.

One morning I was in an irritable mood in general. I'd had a rough couple of weeks and was looking forward to a nice long walk. Being a dog may be tough, but being a human isn't any easier. People can disappoint you. Friendships can turn toxic. People you dearly love can get sick and die. Money can be tight while prices keep rising. All of that's just for starters. I am so grateful for being an upbeat person most of the time. But sometimes things pile up—they can be small things but they add up—and you have to find ways to "reset" your emotional thermostat.

Galaxy's leg had healed; thankfully she wasn't limping anymore. Our morning walks were always a peaceful, quiet bonding time for both of us, which I needed that morning. I decided to stay in the neighborhood, rather than deal with traffic and drive to the park. I could *feel* how short my fuse was and just wanted some time to relax and enjoy the sunshine with my dog.

It was a beautiful spring day in the Mojave Desert, bright and sunny, warm but not yet too hot. Our neighborhood was generally very quiet and very spread out, so there were never many people walking dogs or out at all on any given day.

That was exactly what I wanted. Just some peace and quiet.

So I went and pulled her e-collar from its charger. Galaxy saw me and immediately got up from her spot on the couch, wagging her tail happily. I put the collar on and clipped her leash to her collar. She eagerly followed me, looking forward to the walk as much as I was. It was a nice, perfect day, just the two of us.

Chapter Seventeen

There are leash laws in Clark County, so I always keep Galaxy on a leash, but she stays right by my heel, so I always let it hang loose, holding on to it with just a finger or two, able to tighten my grip on it if I needed to, but just keeping it relaxed as we walked. I was enjoying myself. Galaxy was calm and happy. I was enjoying the picturesque morning, and let my mind wander as we walked.

"Don't bite me!" a voice called.

I'd heard that voice before. It was a neighbor who liked to ride his bike around the neighborhood the same time I'd walk Galaxy. He always repeated that phrase every time he passed us. No "Hi," or "Good morning," or any kind of polite greeting. Just those same three words, every single time. It irritated the hell out of me.

This morning it downright startled me. I jumped and pulled Galaxy close, then rolled my eyes when I saw that it was him.

"Could you knock that off?" I demanded angrily.

He slowed down but still kept a noticeable distance between himself and Galaxy. "Relax, it was just a joke."

"Oh, sure. Next time I see you, I'll just yell, 'Don't rape me!' Then we can see how funny that joke is."

He scoffed. "How about you calm down?"

"How about you knock it off? Quit yelling at me and my dog every time you see us. It's weird. And creepy."

"The heck with you," he replied.

I dropped Galaxy's leash and saw his eyes immediately widen as he realized there was nothing between him and my dog. Nothing to stop her, should she decide to go after him. Of course, she didn't move from my side. She knew I wasn't afraid of this man, and that he didn't pose a threat. I was just pissed off.

"Say that again," I told him. "Say *one* more word to me or my dog, ever again. I *dare* you."

He opened his mouth like he was going to say something, then thought better of it and rode away, shaking his head. I bent down and picked up Galaxy's leash, then petted her for a moment.

Immediately I felt bad. I shouldn't have done that. That was an overreaction, and all it accomplished was to make that guy *more* scared of

Galaxy than he already was. But dammit, I was having a rough day. I'd just had my peaceful walk interrupted. I was *allowed* to be angry and to tell him to knock it off.

As I said to him, it wouldn't be okay for me to randomly walk past him or any innocent man, one minding his own business, doing nothing wrong, and yell, "Don't rape me!"

That would be wrong. Every random guy has the right to exist in public and mind his own business without being bothered. It probably wouldn't make him feel good if I just yelled that at him—for no reason other than the fact that he was existing in the same general area as me. So why did this neighbor think it was okay for him to do that to me and my dog? She hadn't done anything wrong. We were just minding our busi-

Chapter Seventeen

ness, existing outdoors in our neighborhood. I didn't like him constantly saying that to me—every single time I saw him. I wanted him to stop.

It was completely acceptable to tell him to stop. But when he argued, I should have just stayed calm, instead of letting his fear get to me. It was exhausting, sometimes, always having to be the calm one, always having to make sure Galaxy is better behaved, quieter, calmer, more stable than any other kind of dog. The world didn't care that she'd been abused and was fearful and anxious because of it. No one cared that she brought so much joy to all the people she worked with. There was always this expectation that she had to be perfect, all the time, no matter what. Sometimes she wasn't perfect. Sometimes I wasn't perfect either.

There would always be people who were afraid of her. After years of owning her, that was nothing new. But I could probably practice a little more when it came to reacting to that fear. It always hurt the worst, though, when that fear and prejudice came from our friends or family. People who *knew* Galaxy. Especially people who knew her after we'd worked her through her initial fears.

I could understand people being unsure of her right after we got her. She was perfect in the house with us, but even our relatives scared the crap out of her, and she'd bark incessantly at them. In time, my immediate family would come to love her and vice versa, but we had to—and did—spend so much time and effort working her through that. She pushed herself so hard to overcome those irrational fears. Once she did, she was a completely different dog. Unfortunately, we had friends who knew her as the calm, balanced, happy-go-lucky lady that she is and were *still* scared of her. That always hurt a little. It never got any easier to deal with.

We have friends, people that Galaxy knows and likes, who won't even open up our gate if she is out in the yard, just because they are so scared of her. Alan's uncle, to this day, hates her. He's never spent time with her. He's never petted her nor interacted with her. Not once, in all the years we've had her, has he been within ten feet of her. He won't even go into the yard at all while she's outside. That hurts a lot, and it makes me feel unwelcome in Alan's family.

It hurts to know that Alan's uncle will never accept the dog I love—the dog I chose to bring into this family. And it's not because of anything she did, but because of the unfair "bad rap" that pit bulls get. No matter how much you tell people that it's the people, not the dogs that are responsible when things go very, very wrong, the prejudice remains.

Galaxy would bark at people she didn't know, which we liked and never corrected her for doing. We *wanted* her to bark and alert us if someone she didn't know was approaching the gate. But as soon as we walked out, she calmed down. She'd done her job and had alerted the humans, and as soon as she saw us greet the person and let them in, as soon as she knew that particular human was okay, her focus turned instantly to doing everything in her power to convince them to pet her for literally the rest of her life.

Our lawn maintenance guys often opened up the gate while she was outside. She'd learned long ago that they were allowed in the yard, and would run happily to greet them and move from one to the other, wanting constant attention. Finally, I'd hear their voices and walk out to see Galaxy lying on her back, her tail wagging madly as a grown man rubbed her belly and spoke to her in a high, happy voice.

That was my favorite thing about her. As I discussed earlier, she seemed to especially inspire softness in men, the bigger and tougher looking the better. Maybe tough-on-the-outside men felt more comfortable being openly affectionate with a dog that looks as tough as Galaxy does. It never failed to bring a smile to my face whenever I walked out and saw these big, muscle-bound men, well accustomed to doing manual labor in the scorching desert heat, using baby talk with her.

It was adorable, and I loved that she brought that out in so many men. In a world that doesn't always let men feel comfortable showing affection, or express feelings of cuteness, I liked seeing Galaxy bring that out in them. I always felt bad calling her inside when she was having so much fun with the yard guys. But if I didn't, she'd constantly be in their way, begging for attention, and they'd never get anything done.

They came by a couple of days after the incident with the cyclist. When I heard them outside, I went out to greet them.

"Good morning," I said.

Chapter Seventeen

They looked up from petting Galaxy, who had sat down literally on top of the oldest guy's feet, leaning heavily against him so he could pet her face and chest.

"Good morning," he replied. "This is a sweet dog."

"Some people don't agree," I answered, relaying the story about the cycling neighbor. All three of the men laughed.

"Yeah, she's terrifying," the youngest man said.

"Well, sure she is," the older man replied, kneeling. "Look at this big scary face."

His kneeling made Galaxy's entire day. She stood up and turned to face him, enthusiastically licking him all over his face.

"Oh, no!" he cried. "I'm being mauled! Look, she's mauling me!"

This made Galaxy even happier, and she wiggled her entire body, prancing on her front legs, as if to say, "Yes! Yes, this is such a fun game!"

The man leaned back against the iron fence, and Galaxy moved even closer, practically lying on top of him, still trying to lick any skin she could reach.

"Oh, the horror!" the man exclaimed. "The horror! Such a vicious mauling!"

Finally, he looked back up at me with a grin, wiping his face. "Yeah, you gotta be careful, man," he said. "She's a killer, that one. I'll be scarred for life."

The third man had moved to stand beside me while we watched the older guy play with Galaxy. "People are idiots," he told me. "The first time I came here, I was intimidated as hell. No point even trying to lie about it. She's a big dog, and she's got a *look*, you know?"

"Yeah, that's true," I had to agree.

"But I mean, look at that." He gestured to Galaxy and his coworker. "That's just not an aggressive dog. We've seen plenty of aggressive dogs, and we've got some customers we have to call before we go in, to make sure the dogs are kept inside. But that's not an aggressive dog. She just wants to love on folks."

"Yeah, that's true."

"Some people will always be stupid. You're always going to have people judging her by how she looks. You can't control that. But she's a good dog. That's the only thing that matters."

Chapter Eighteen

After Galaxy received the all clear from the vet, she was so excited to go back to work. When she saw the vest come out, after almost a month of not seeing it, she behaved like an excited puppy. She jumped up and spun around, absolutely ecstatic. Once I got it buckled on her, she pranced impatiently at the door, as if she wasn't in any pain at all. When we pulled up to the nursing home, she kept whining from the back seat, wanting nothing more than to be let out of the car so she could run in and be petted by every single person in the building. That in itself made my heart soar. This was something that brought her so much love and so much joy.

That first day back, Galaxy hurried down her ramp and stared expectantly at me as I folded it up and put it back in the car. It must have felt to her like I was taking forever, but I finally got the car closed and locked, and we walked into the building. Well, *I* walked, anyway. Galaxy, on the other hand, *pranced*. The doors slid open, and I swear she thought she was strolling down a red carpet, smiling and posing and stopping to let everyone admire her. She looked like a damn movie star, the way she moved. She was back in her element, and she loved it.

We made our rounds and saw Dan, the same lonely old man we'd seen on our first visit. Every time we came here we always made sure to stop by his room, or hunt him down if he was somewhere else. Sometimes I tried to save him for last, so we could spend a little extra time with him.

Today was one of those days. We found him in his room, sitting in a wheelchair, watching TV.

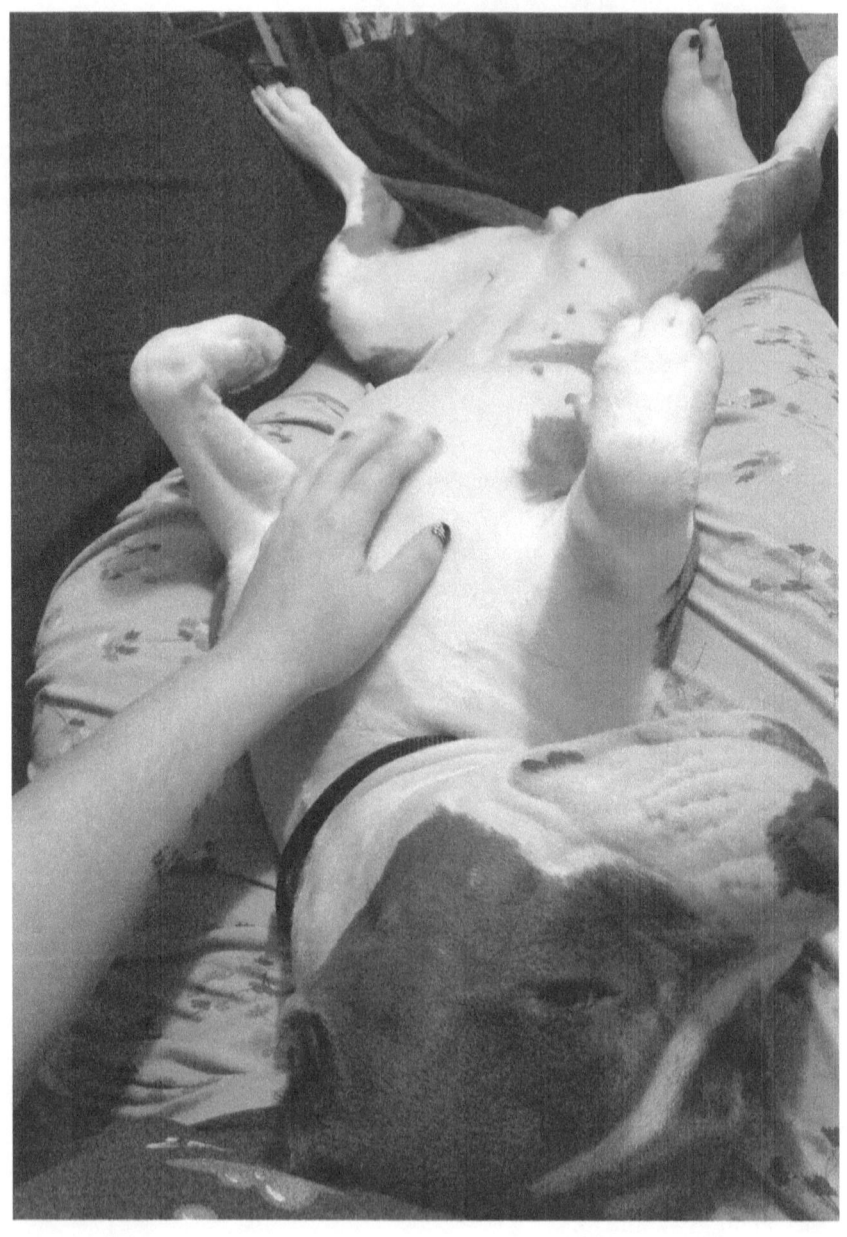

Chapter Eighteen

"Good morning," I greeted him from the doorway. "Would you like a therapy dog visit today?"

He still seemed mostly shut down and didn't respond when people spoke to him. He could hear just fine; he just usually didn't care. But by now he'd spent time with us regularly over the years and instantly recognized my voice.

"The dog," he murmured, reaching out for Galaxy. I gave her the leash and let her lead the way in.

She loved Dan. He was one of her favorite patients. She seemed to enjoy his quiet nature, and she'd just sit there in silence, her head in his lap, sighing contentedly as he petted her and told her, over and over, what a good dog she was.

I always loved seeing him with her. I didn't know anything about him, aside from his name. But I could always see how lonely he was. How he was just done with the world, and wanted nothing to do with it. Galaxy was one of the few things on the planet that could get a reaction out of him. The nurses and aides who worked with him gave me the impression that he was very lucid, just in a lot of pain. I didn't know why, and I knew they couldn't tell me details about their patients, so I just accepted him as he was, and let him spend time with Galaxy.

He never really talked to me. Never asked my name, never even asked Galaxy's name. He never told me about the dog he once had, which he still missed very much. Occasionally I'd hear him whisper, "I miss my dog. I want a dog," but it always felt like he was talking more to Galaxy than to me.

In truth, he'd never acknowledge me at all, until it was time to leave. Every once in a while he'd ask us to stay a little longer, but usually, he would just be quiet and watch us walk away. It always broke my heart. Leaving him never got any easier. So I always wanted to give him a little extra time if I could.

And Galaxy adored him every bit as much as he adored her. She never got bored with him, she never expected anything from him, she'd just look up at him with the softest expression in her calm brown eyes. And he'd stroke her, his gnarled and arthritic hands gentle and tender as he ran his fingers along her face, over her ears, along her neck. A definite bond had grown between them, and the familiarity they had with each other was beautiful.

I waited as long as we could, then I thanked him for his time, and Galaxy dutifully followed me out of the room. It was so bittersweet leaving his room. On the one hand, I loved being able to give him those few moments of companionship and was so grateful that Galaxy could do that for him. But on the other, it meant that it would likely be a week or two before we'd see him again. His kids and grandkids lived on the other side of the country. He didn't get many visitors.

So, just a few days later, when I got a call at 10 p.m. from the volunteer coordinator at the nursing home, I didn't need him to say a word. I knew exactly what was going on, and exactly why he was calling. Dan was dying. He only had a few hours left, and his family wasn't going to be there in time.

"He always asks to see Galaxy," the coordinator told me. "We could have a volunteer sit with him and talk to him, but I think he'd feel better if she was there."

He didn't need to say anything else. I was already putting on my shoes and reaching for Galaxy's leash. "We'll be there in twenty minutes," I told him.

Alan walked into the room just as I hung up. "What's going on?" he asked, concerned.

"Dan's dying. His family is too far away, so he's alone."

Alan's face fell. "Oh, damn," he whispered. "That's . . . damn, that's rough."

"Yeah, they don't have anyone to sit with him. The coordinator asked if I'd bring Galaxy and stay with him."

"Until he dies?"

"Yeah."

He seemed hesitant. "Will you be okay with that?" he asked. "I know you like him a lot."

I smiled, flattered that he was worried about me. "I'll be fine," I assured him. "You're right; I do like him. That's why I *want* to be there."

He nodded. "I'll wait up until you get home."

I smiled again. "Thank you, sweetheart."

Chapter Eighteen

Galaxy was excited, of course. She saw the vest come out. It always made her excited. But she was also a little confused. We'd never gone to work at night before. I'm sure she could sense something different about my energy.

Honestly, though, I wasn't upset. I wasn't sad. I felt *determined*. I *wanted* to be there. They told me that he could pass any time, between right this moment and a few hours from now. I wanted to make sure we were there in time. This was someone Galaxy loved. Someone she'd bonded with. There was absolutely no doubt in my mind that she would want to be there every bit as much as I did.

We pulled into the empty parking lot and saw a nurse standing in the lobby with the coordinator.

"Do I need to sign in?" I asked them.

"No, we'll do that later," the nurse told me. "Come with me."

Her face was grim. She nodded once to the volunteer coordinator and began walking quickly through the halls.

"Have you ever lost a relative?" she asked me.

"Uh, yeah. I was there when my dad died a few years back."

"So you're aware of Cheyne-Stokes?"

"That's the breathing they do, right?"

Oh, yes. I was aware of that. It had been jarring to see at first, but the doctors and nurses assured me that the gasping, rattling, irregular breathing wasn't a sign that they were in pain. It was just potentially distressing to see.

"You might want to talk to him," she continued. "Tell him stories, whatever."

"Can he still hear me?"

"We think so, yes."

I glanced down at Galaxy. She seemed to have some kind of understanding of what was going on. She strode through the hall with a definite purpose, her head and tail down, as if she were looking for Dan. There was none of her usual happy-go-lucky cheerfulness, but just that desire to find him.

It occurred to me how big she was. "Where do you want her?" I asked the nurse. "Just next to the bed?"

The nurse glanced around as if to make sure no one else was within earshot. But the place was empty and dimly lit. "No," she whispered. "Another nurse is waiting in the room. We're going to lift the dog and let her sit next to him on the bed."

"Really?"

Generally, with big dogs, that was *not* allowed. Even with how gentle Galaxy was, she was still seventy pounds of solid muscle, and some of these patients were quite frail. It wouldn't take much for her to accidentally hurt someone.

"As long as she remains calm while lifting her, yes," the nurse told me. "I've heard that she's very calm. That's correct?"

"Yes, she's very gentle."

"Then the risk is low enough that we're willing to take it."

The nurse's eyes, which had been sharp with an intense focus, softened. "Dan's been here, by himself, for too long. I always know which days you visited, because he talks about the dog for hours. He deserves to be able to spend his last moments with her."

We reached the door to his room. Usually, Galaxy knows to stop and wait for permission from the patient to enter, but this time she didn't so much as slow down. She walked right in, ignoring the male nurse standing inside, and went straight for the bed.

"Hey, look, Dan," the nurse said. "You've got a visitor. Do you know this young lady's name?"

"Her name is Galaxy," I chimed in.

Galaxy ignored both of us. She stood up on her hind legs and put her front paws on the edge of the bed, sniffing Dan's hand.

"How do you want to lift her?" the nurse asked the woman, who seemed to be the supervisor.

It took some brainstorming, but we figured out how to get Galaxy up onto the bed. At first, she stood above him, her face directly above his, just watching him breathing. That's when it seemed to sink in for her—what was happening. She gave a soft whine, a sound I'd never heard her make before or since, then tenderly moved to lie beside him, careful not to step on him. The nurse moved Dan's arm out from his side and rested

Chapter Eighteen

it on top of Galaxy's head. He then gave Galaxy a reassuring pet. "That's it, old girl," he told her. "You know exactly what's going on, don't you?"

Then he turned to me. "I'll be at that desk, right outside in the hall," he told me. "Just call me if you need anything. I'll be by every few minutes to check on you."

I thanked him, and both nurses left. I was alone with a dying man. The supervisor had suggested I talk to him, but now I found myself unsure of what to say.

"Do you mind if I put on some music?" I asked, knowing he wouldn't answer. But the silence, broken only by his labored breathing, felt oppressive. I grabbed my phone, pulled up my playlists, and picked a compilation of soft, gentle music.

I let the music on my phone play softly. Then I turned back to Dan, still looking for something to say. Suddenly, I felt so unsure of myself. I would be the last person to speak to this man, the last human voice he'd ever hear. And Galaxy would be the last soul he would truly connect with before he passed.

It felt big. Too big, for someone like me. It occurred to me that I didn't know him. I wish I had. So finally, I decided to just tell him that.

"I wish I'd known you when you were younger," I told him. "I wish I'd been able to meet your dog. But I'm glad you got to meet mine. Did you know, the first time we met you was her very first day as a therapy dog?"

I told him about that woman in the store, who had changed our lives by showing me what Galaxy was capable of doing. I told him about Galaxy's past, the abuse she endured, the injuries that still plague her, and the pain and fear she still lived with every day. I told him how profound it was to meet that woman in the store, how her face would forever be burned into my memory, and how Galaxy had known just what to do and how to be.

I told him about Martina, who had been hesitant. Who, the same morning I met him, had given me so much grief and made me feel like I didn't belong there. I told him how grateful I was to have met him, and to have seen how Galaxy had been able to connect with him. How it had reaffirmed my belief that we *did* belong there, that Galaxy was born for this. I laughed as I told him how speechless I was after the visit when

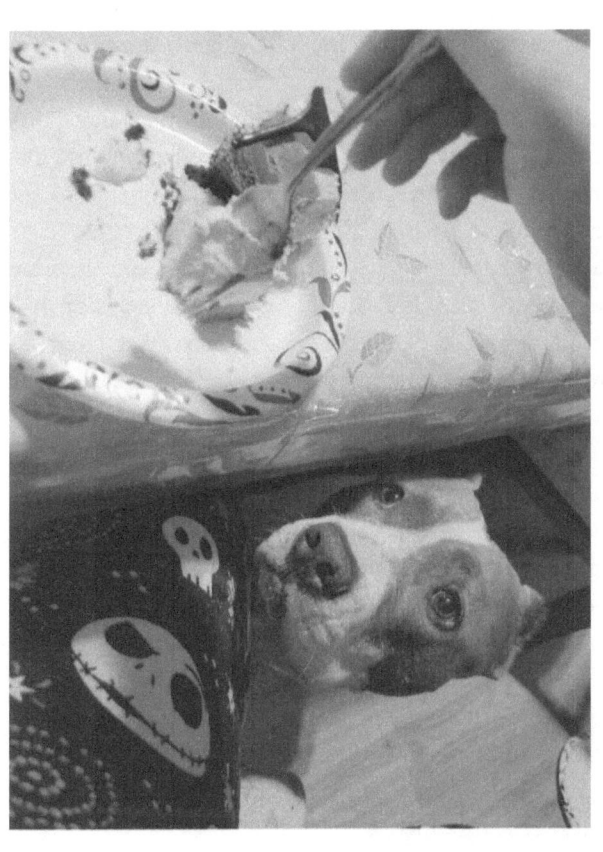

Martina had reminded me that not everyone would be welcoming and that I couldn't take it personally.

For two hours I talked to him, telling him stories about Galaxy, this abandoned and unwanted dog that had been through hell and come out the other side. Galaxy never moved, not once. She never readjusted to get comfortable, she never scratched an itch, and she never had to pee.

She didn't even acknowledge me as I talked about her. She just lay there, her back against Dan's side, her body lying right alongside his, offering that silent, steady comfort. She knew exactly what was happening, and what we were doing there. She knew what her job was, and that was the only thing she cared about. I knew, somehow, just by watching her that it didn't matter how long it took. She was going to stay right there, right at that moment with Dan, for every moment he had left. He was her friend. She understood him, she knew him, in a way I never would. She had seen into his heart and found gold. It didn't matter who he was in the past. It didn't matter what kind of life he led. Galaxy didn't need to know any of that to be there with him at that moment.

He stopped breathing for a worryingly long time but then gasped for air. His time was getting close.

I sighed. "She's going to miss you," I told him. "You're her friend. We're never going to forget you. She's going to carry a part of you with her, always. You helped her. You helped *us*."

Then I fell into a comfortable silence. There was nothing left to say and nothing left to tell him—this man I barely knew, and never had the chance to get to know.

Galaxy didn't mind the silence. She lay there, still and quiet, until finally, after a long few minutes, he breathed out and didn't breathe in again.

Galaxy lifted her head to look over at him. She was still for a moment, then sat up, sniffing him and whining softly. I called for the nurse, and he appeared a few seconds later. Galaxy didn't move. She just stayed right there, sitting in Dan's bed, next to him, staring at him and whimpering softly.

The nurse walked in and sighed, then put an affectionate hand on Dan's leg. "See you later, man," he said quietly. He looked at Galaxy, still

Chapter Eighteen

sitting there, and reached out to pet her. "It's all right, girl." She didn't respond to him talking to her or touching her, but just whined again, this time a little louder. "Hey, it's all right. It's okay. He's not hurting anymore. You're okay, girl. Come on, let's get you down." She watched Dan for another second, then finally stood up so that the nurse could help me lift her off the bed and put her on the ground. But immediately she stood back up, her front paws on the bed, and rested her head on Dan's lifeless hand. It broke my heart to watch.

Galaxy had been there, right there, with him through his last moments, and she'd gotten to say goodbye. It had been a peaceful moment, just her and him. But now, as I watched her mourning her friend, my heart broke for her. "It's all right, baby," I murmured, moving to her side. "Come on, get down."

She obeyed and moved to stand right next to me, leaning heavily against me for comfort as she said goodbye to her friend for the very last time. The nurse offered his hand to her, and she moved to him, wanting affection. "It's all right," he told her. "Hey, it's all right. You're okay, old girl. You did good."

We got home, and I was completely drained. As promised, Alan was there, waiting for me, when we walked through the door.

"Hey," he said, standing up from where he'd been lounging on the couch. "Is . . . is he gone?"

"Yeah."

"Are you okay?"

I sighed. "Yeah, I think so," I told him.

He walked up to me and gave me a long, comforting hug. "Are you sure?"

"Yeah," I said. "It was sad, but he's not hurting anymore. I'm glad we went. I wouldn't have wanted him to die alone."

Alan turned his attention to Galaxy and knelt to pet her. "How is she?" he asked.

"She's okay. Kind of quiet. But she did great. She had lain right by his side the entire time. It was sweet to watch. But she was sad right after he died. I think she was grieving him."

"She's known him for a while," he agreed. "I'm glad she got to say goodbye, instead of just never seeing him again."

"Me, too. And I'm glad that we could be there for him."

He looked down and petted her as she sat at his feet. "But maybe tomorrow you can take her to the pet store or the coffee shop or something, and get her a treat. Just something to make her feel a little better, you know?"

I nodded. "That's a good idea."

But the next morning when I woke up, Galaxy was back to her normal self. She'd dealt with her sadness, and then she moved on.

I liked that. I liked that she was able to do her job and provide comfort to someone who needed it; she seemed to be at peace with knowing she'd done everything she could and her friend wasn't suffering anymore.

She had been with her friend during the last moments of his life and had *truly* been right there with him. He would have wanted her to move on now, and be happy. He loved her, and he would have wanted her to have lots of treats, love, and affection. So I may have spent a little more than usual at the pet store. It turned into almost a ritual, giving her things I knew Dan would have wanted her to have. He would've loved to see her sniffing around the shelves, choosing her new plushies and chew toys. He would've loved to see how excited she was when I got her back in the car and opened up one of the packages of her favorite treats.

Dan got to say goodbye to her, and I knew how much he loved her and that he would have wanted to make sure she was every bit as happy as she made him.

That's a good dog, he used to tell me.

Yes, she very much was, and I would always make sure she knew it.

Chapter Nineteen

As the weather warmed up, Galaxy was back to her goofy, happy-go-lucky self. Alan had a new job that required a lot of overtime, so Aaron and I were sitting at home one weekend, bored out of our minds. I groaned when I checked the time on my phone and saw that it wasn't even 10 a.m. yet. This would be a long day of doing absolutely nothing interesting. I looked over to Aaron as he mindlessly scrolled through videos on his phone. It was obvious he wasn't thrilled about being bored any more than I was.

"You want to go hiking?" I asked him.

He perked up immediately. "Where?" he asked.

I could tell by his expression what he was thinking. "Not Death Valley," I said before he could ask. "How about Red Rock?"

His expression fell, but only slightly. And I couldn't fault him for it.

Death Valley National Park, my absolute favorite place in the world, and one of Aaron's favorites, too, was a two-hour drive away, but Red Rock Canyon was not even a half hour's drive. As a bonus, dogs are allowed in Red Rock, while they aren't allowed on any trails in Death Valley, so Galaxy could come with us.

We packed some water, loaded Galaxy into the car, and drove off. We had a great time, and when we got out of the car we were delighted to find that the temperature was incredibly pleasant, with a slight breeze that helped keep things cool.

Weekends were usually busy at Red Rock, but this time there were only a couple of other cars parked at the trailhead. This was perfect. With a beautiful day, and not a lot of other people around, we'd be able to enjoy the outdoors. I clipped Galaxy's leash and set up her ramp so she could get out of the car.

As I did, a car driving by on the road stopped, and the window rolled down. "Is that an American Bully?" a woman called to me from the driver's seat.

I turned. "We think so," I shouted back.

"She's beautiful! I've got two of my own at home. They're great dogs!"

I smiled at her, casting a glance down the road. It was quiet, so there was little chance of anyone driving up behind her, but I found it funny that she'd stopped her car in the middle of the road to have a conversation about Bullies.

"She's a cuddle bug!" Aaron shouted, wanting to join in.

The woman nodded. "Oh, yes, they love people!"

I bit my lip to keep from grinning as Aaron and the woman continued shouting to each other across the empty parking lot, while the woman stayed right there on the main road. It was the cutest and dumbest thing I'd ever seen.

What other breed causes a reaction like that? How many other breeds inspire random people to stop their moving vehicles on a road to start shouting a conversation across a parking lot about how awesome the breed is, and how misunderstood they are?

Aaron, of course, loved it. He always loves any chance he can get to talk about his dog—and Galaxy *is his* dog, which he is always very quick to point out.

I listened to them shout to each other about how awesome pit bull types are, and while part of me was very concerned about the possibility of someone driving up behind her, I thought it was so sweet of her to do that. She was a woman who loved these dogs—so much so that even the sight of one made her want to offer compliments to us about ours.

After the conversation ended and the woman drove away, I smiled down at Aaron. "Ready?" I asked.

"Yeah. That lady was really nice."

"She was, wasn't she?"

"Her dogs sound like they were nice, too."

"Yeah, they do."

Chapter Nineteen

We walked along the empty trail, just enjoying the quiet. But the deeper we went into the canyon, the more we could hear the faint sound of falling water.

"Do you hear that?" Aaron asked, after about a half hour of walking.

"I hear it. It sounds like water."

"Is there water near here?"

"Maybe."

I didn't tell him that the trail we were hiking ended at a seasonal waterfall. Living in the desert, waterfalls were generally pretty rare, and only showed up in the spring, after a snowy winter. I didn't want to get his hopes up that we would see one, and then be disappointed if it wasn't there. But as we got closer, I could hear it.

We squeezed through a particularly narrow gap between two massive boulders and found ourselves in an empty valley, surrounded by high cliffs. Sure enough, there was the waterfall. Well, *waterfall* is a strong word. It was more of a trickle, but still impressive enough that Aaron audibly gasped.

We sat down on a rock, and I pulled some snacks out of the backpack I was carrying. I also pulled out Galaxy's collapsible portable water bowl and let her drink her fill. There was a little creek at the bottom, fed by the waterfall, and she sniffed around at the edge of the water, curious, but too timid to get her paws wet. No, she was much more comfortable sitting by my side, drinking filtered water out of her bowl.

After a few minutes of rest and a few more minutes of letting Aaron play, we packed up our things, collected our trash, and started the hike back. At one point, I saw a beautiful rock outcrop. I turned to Aaron.

"Why don't you sit right there, and I can get a picture of you and Galaxy together."

"Sure," he said, moving to sit down in front of the rock. I sat Galaxy down beside him, then moved back to take the photo. I heard other people walking up as I took the picture, but didn't pay any attention to them until one woman spoke up. "Would you like me to take a picture with all three of you?" she asked.

I looked over to see a group of five or six adults walking along the trail. I straightened up and smiled at the woman.

"That would be amazing. Thank you," I said, handing her the phone.

I moved to sit beside Aaron while the woman took the photo for us. She even made kissing sounds to get Galaxy's attention, which I thought was a sweet touch.

After she took the picture I stood up, grabbed Galaxy's leash, and approached the woman for my phone. "Thank you. I appreciate that," I told her, as one of the men in her group called Galaxy over to him, so he could pet her.

She chuckled. "Oh, I'm a mom, too," she told me. "I know what it's like to always be the one taking the pictures, and never be in them. But those two youngsters looked so pretty sitting there. I knew you had to be in it, too."

Galaxy was happy to move along with each person in the group, eagerly wanting attention. I thought it was funny, as I watched her, and as Aaron answered questions about her. Again I recalled that this was the same dog that, when we first got her, barked in the most terrified, high-pitched, squeaky voice whenever strange people got too close. The same dog that would have been a nervous, neurotic wreck standing in the middle of a group of strangers, with all of them bent over her, talking to her and petting her.

She was still scared and timid around unfamiliar things, sure. But *people*, well, she learned a long time ago that people have hands that give her pets and treats, and now her entire life goal revolved around being petted by humans every waking moment.

"She was abused," Aaron was explaining, having been asked about her crooked ears. "Her first owners cut off her ears with scissors."

"Oh, that's awful!"

"People are jerks," one of the men added. He lifted his head to look at Aaron. "Good on you for rescuing her."

Aaron grinned and then had to tell the story about how when we were at the shelter we had been interested in a *different* dog, but then we found Galaxy—or maybe she found us! We chatted for a moment more, then said our goodbyes and continued down the path. Soon after, we turned a corner and saw our car in the parking lot.

"What did you think?" I asked him. "Did you have fun?"

Chapter Nineteen

"Yeah. The people we saw today were nice."

"They were. And I'm glad it wasn't too crowded."

I loaded Galaxy and the kid into the car and started driving home. Before I was even out of the park, they were both asleep. It was a good thing that the woman had offered to take that picture of us, and good that I'd thought to grab a couple of pictures of Aaron and Galaxy. They were the last pictures we ever took of Galaxy while hiking.

Chapter Twenty

As the months went on, the more we took Galaxy out walking or on hikes with us, the more of a problem it was becoming. I ended up taking her to the vet two more times in three months because of persistent limping. At first, it wasn't too difficult to manage. We changed her diet and put her on different joint health supplements, as well as painkillers for the bad days. It didn't solve the problem completely but helped make her daily life a little more manageable. But I started to notice her personality change, just a bit, because of the pain she was constantly feeling.

Part of it was good. Galaxy had always had a bit of a prey drive and was the terror of all the wild jackrabbits in our yard. Now, her prey drive was diminishing to almost nothing, which, all in all, didn't bother me. Of course, she was always too clumsy and too slow to ever catch anything, though she did once get in a fight with a stray cat that had gotten into our yard. She lost that fight, and it became one of our favorite running jokes. Of all the pit bulls in the world, we found the one that got her ass handed to her by a cat. So I wasn't too upset to see her prey drive diminishing. I'm sure the wild rabbits were happy about that as well.

But the main thing, the biggest personality change, was her lack of patience and tolerance for other dogs. Humans, though, she still loved and wanted to be around all the time. Every new human was still a potential best friend, and her goal was still to see how long she could convince any given human to pet her.

It was just dogs.

A year before, she'd been fine with most other dogs, as long as they didn't get in her space before she was ready. She'd readily played with them in dog parks and sniffed them and wanted to meet them all. But now she was losing her patience with them.

She wasn't dog reactive, as long as they were on a leash and kept their distance. She never barked or growled. But if they got too close, she'd snap at them.

Maybe her patience was diminishing. Maybe she was worried about her ability to defend herself while being in pain. Maybe she felt too vulnerable. Whatever the reason, she had less patience than she had in her younger years. Even so, it was mild. So when we took her hiking with us, we'd always simply move to the side of the trail to let the other dogs pass, and Galaxy certainly didn't mind taking a break now and then.

We stuck with the easier trails, and she always had so much fun, just out enjoying nature. But often, on the way back to the car, we started to notice that she'd always move very slowly, not looking around, not showing much enjoyment at all. The poor girl was in pain, and Alan and I finally had to face the fact that she was just not healthy enough for hikes anymore. All it was doing was making her pain worse.

Chapter Twenty

Besides, we still had our daily walks. Galaxy was always much more relaxed on those anyway. We had our favorite park that we'd go to, and she'd spend time watching the geese that lived there or just relaxing in the grass in between walking laps around the park. But then, for about a month, she started showing the same signs of pain during our walks that she had on our hikes: moving slowly, limping, stiff joints, not looking around or seeming to enjoy herself.

Finally, even that had to stop. None of the treatments we tried had any effect. She was only eight years old, but her mobility was becoming a problem. Aging her, robbing her of her youth and energy, far too quickly.

"What about her work?" Alan asked. "Does she limp when you take her to work?"

"Sometimes, yeah."

"Do you think it's time for her to retire?"

I hesitated. I didn't like the idea of taking away this thing she loved doing.

"Not quite yet," I said. "But it's probably going to have to happen soon."

The more I saw her limp in the yard and watched her stiffly move every morning, the more I realized that we were quickly approaching the point where we'd need to seriously consider retiring her. This was just causing her so much pain. Yet she still loved it, and that's what made the decision so difficult.

Over the next few weeks, I started watching her more closely during our therapy dog visits, looking for signs that she was ready to retire. She never showed any. This was something she still loved, still took so much enjoyment in, and looked forward to, even when she was limping or moving a little more slowly. But I felt so guilty like I was pushing her to work through her pain. I found myself wrestling with when to retire her. It didn't help that I took so much enjoyment from her work as well.

Was I just trying to encourage her to push through her pain to satisfy my ego? Was I making her pain worse because *I* liked the feeling it gave me to see her interact with her patients? Was I being silly and judging myself too harshly for wanting her to continue doing something she loves, for as long as she can? Would it be worse to take away something she truly enjoyed and could still do, despite her physical pain? When would it be "the right time" for her to retire? Should I retire her *now*, while she still has some mobility left? Or should I wait, knowing that all the walking could potentially be making her condition worse?

What would she choose, if it were up to her?

I'd known for a long time that this day would eventually come, and I'd tried my hardest to brace myself for it. That it was here now—that her pain was causing problems—didn't make anything any easier.

I realized that there *was* no right answer. No matter what happened, her mobility problems weren't going to get any better. It's not like she was ever unhappy with lounging around on the couch or snuggling in our laps. She had a good home life, a family who loved her, and plenty of treats and affection. So maybe it was okay to go ahead and retire her now. After spending the last four years helping other people, it was okay if now we switched our focus to helping *her* and making her comfortable while she could still get around.

Finally, I made my decision. We'd retire her on a high note, give her a great last visit, and let her just be a spoiled, pampered house pet for the rest of her life. I called the volunteer coordinator at the nursing home to let them know this would be our last visit. It was a fight, during the whole drive over, to keep my emotions under control. This was going to be the last time I'd ever make this drive.

Galaxy was completely immune to the sadness I felt. She was just enjoying the car ride, enjoying the beautiful summer day.

We walked into the front lobby and checked in with the volunteer coordinator.

"It's good to see you," he said cheerfully as he handed me my volunteer sticker. "There's a small gathering in the cafeteria. Why don't I walk you there?"

I was confused. I'd been there hundreds of times. I knew where the cafeteria was. But the coordinator just seemed so eager that I didn't want to disappoint him. We followed him down the hall and into the cafeteria, and my heart skipped a beat.

As soon as they saw us in the hall, dozens of people suddenly started cheering. I blinked, surprised, and maybe a little overwhelmed, to see that

Chapter Twenty

the room was full of patients and staff, balloons, food, and a big banner that said, "Thank you, Galaxy!"

For a moment, I just stood there, my mind blank as I took in everything. Galaxy, of course, was *ecstatic* to be getting all of this attention, people clapping for her and cheering her name.

"We decided to throw you a surprise party!" the coordinator told me. "Come on in!"

I was still dumbfounded, still speechless, as I followed him into the room. Suddenly at least a dozen pairs of hands were all there, reaching out for Galaxy. And good lord, seeing her react, realizing that all those hands were petting *her*, it was the best freaking day of her entire life. She instantly sank and rolled onto her back for belly rubs, her tail whipping madly back and forth, her tongue lolling out of her mouth as she lay there with her silly pit bull grin.

"This can't be for us," I heard myself say.

One of the aides walked up and clapped me on my shoulder. "Of course it is," he assured me. "Galaxy has been such a great friend to everyone here; we figured she deserves a proper retirement party. And here, look, Gwen has something for you."

He moved to the side so a woman sitting in the wheelchair behind him could hold something out for me.

"I crocheted her a scarf," Gwen told me, holding out a collar that had been crocheted out of soft yarn.

I'm not a crier. I don't cry pretty much ever. But tears stung the backs of my eyes as I thanked her and took the gift.

"Thank you, this means . . . it means a lot," I said, my voice shaking.

Gwen beckoned me to come closer. "Don't ever let anyone tell you what kind of dog she is," she murmured. "We know what kind of dog she is, and what kind of person you are. I know you're going to take very good care of her."

"I am."

She smiled at me. "That's a girl. Now move, I want to pet Galaxy. Here, Galaxy, come, girl."

Hearing someone call her name caught Galaxy's attention, and she stood up to move closer to the woman.

"That's my lovely little girl," Gwen cooed, caressing Galaxy's face. "Now you listen here, young lady. I don't want you giving your mama any grief from now on, you understand me? You be a good girl for your mama."

Galaxy just grinned, as if she were saying, "Yes! I am a very good girl! Yes, I am!"

One by one, each patient stopped to take the time to say some kind words to both me and Galaxy. By the end, I was bawling.

We ended up staying a little longer than we usually stayed during our sessions, just socializing, eating delicious food, and having fun with the patients. They all shared hilarious stories from their youth and gave me so much encouragement and love that it was overwhelming. Finally, it was time to leave. I told everyone goodbye. We made one more round so that everyone could get in one last pet, and walked back to my car.

I pulled out my phone from the glove box and saw that Alan had called me a couple of times. Probably wondering why I wasn't back yet. I called him.

"Hey, babe," he said. "Everything okay?"

That was it. I started bawling again as I told him about the surprise party, everything the patients had said, and all the kindness they shared.

"Oh, wow," he said after I'd finished sobbing my way through. "That's one hell of a send-off. How many other dogs can say they got a retirement party?"

I laughed. "It was special."

"Did Galaxy have fun?"

"There were tons of people petting her, all at once. I think her brain short-circuited at one point. She had all these people rubbing her belly at the same time. I don't think I've ever seen *any* animal that happy."

He chuckled over the phone. "That's good. I'm glad you both enjoyed yourselves."

I got home, and Galaxy promptly plopped down on the cool tile and took a nice, long, well-deserved nap. The old girl had had a very big day.

Chapter Twenty-One

In the weeks after retiring Galaxy, I realized that I'd had no reason to worry. She settled easily into her new sedentary life, lounging and sleeping. She still got to go to the pet store and places like that with us, so as far as she was concerned her life was good. I'd made peace with my decision to focus on making her comfortable. I still took her to the park, but now we spent our time relaxing, rather than walking laps.

One afternoon, we pulled up to the park with our big picnic blanket and some snacks to enjoy—and oats so Aaron could feed the geese. I stayed with Galaxy on the blanket while Alan took Aaron to feed the birds. Galaxy didn't mind waiting with me. She lay down, her body right next to mine, her eyes half closed, just enjoying the mild breeze. When they got back, she stood up to greet Alan and Aaron with tail wags and sloppy kisses, then settled down again with all of us.

At one point, Aaron turned so he could lay his head on Galaxy's side, and Galaxy gave a big, contented sigh. I realized, as I watched the two of them cuddling on the picnic blanket, that this felt *good*. Yes, I still missed visiting with all the patients who knew and loved us, and parts of me mourned the loss of that phase of our lives. I found myself mourning the fact that she can't help people anymore like she used to. But she had spent *years* focusing on other people, working through her pain, bringing smiles and joy to everyone who saw her. She'd spent *years* healing broken hearts and giving lonely souls someone to connect with.

Now, it was okay if we wanted to spend the rest of her time focused on her. She still had so much life left to live, and so much love to give to us. I felt grateful for the opportunity to return it.

After a career spent helping so many people, it was time for her to relax and let us help her. This, in all honesty, she was *completely* fine with. Spending the rest of her life pampered and spoiled with love and attention? There is no version of that she wouldn't love.

There were still people who feared her or didn't like her. There will always be people who judge her by her breed. But she'd done her job, she'd changed a lot of hearts and minds, and now she could rest, knowing that she left an impact on the world.

She'd helped the woman in the grocery store. She'd been there to help the gravely injured young veteran who refused to even touch her at first. She'd changed Martina's mind. She'd given Dan another soul to connect with, and given him companionship in his last hours.

Galaxy was no stranger to pain, fear, anxiety, or the cruelty that people are capable of. She'd seen the absolute *worst* of humanity, she'd been the victim of the worst of us, and she'd seen firsthand the evil that we are capable of. But she'd also seen us, I think, at our best. She'd seen a pit bull attack victim push through her fear, choosing love instead of prejudice.

Chapter Twenty-One

She'd seen an angry vet push through the bitterness and rage that had left him shut down. She'd seen an elderly couple bicker playfully with each other while they showered her with attention.

She'd seen another pit bull attack victim, a teenager, push through her fear with strength and determination that left me in awe of that young girl. She's seen a young man defend her, and then pet her in the aisle of a Home Depot, completely unafraid, even though she'd been so agitated only moments before. She'd seen an entire nursing home come together to throw a party for her, for a dog, because she touched every single one of them *that* profoundly. Galaxy had seen us, all of us, from one extreme to the other, from the absolute worst to the best. She'd seen all these people and touched our lives, and changed them for the better.

She's *seen* us. She's judged our hearts. In them, in us, such imperfect creatures, she found something worth loving. Worth protecting. Worth devoting her entire life to nurturing. There's no higher praise than that for a living being—on four legs or two. I've learned from Galaxy that there is much room for improvement—that we can love each other better. We can forgive each other better. We can make room for others who aren't perfect, who maybe need a little extra help. We can accept ourselves, and accept a little extra help if we need it. We can practice the kind of patience and compassion that Galaxy has shown every day of her life—and continues to show to every human who crosses her path—and will continue to do so. So far, no one she has encountered in her "retirement" has betrayed her trust. Today, on an informal basis, she knows who needs an extra dose of her; she goes right up to them, sits on their feet, and gazes into their eyes. No one ever leaves her presence the same.

While I don't step on anyone's feet to keep them from walking away while I silently say to them "I see you; I'm here; you're not alone," the lessons Galaxy taught me have deeply enriched my life and changed the way I interact with everyone who crosses my path—family, friends, and strangers alike.

I hope her story has had an impact on you.

Meet the Authors

Jen Wilson was born in Las Vegas, Nevada. She currently drives an eighteen-wheeler semitruck on long hauls from her home base of Las Vegas. She is the proud wife of Alan and mother of two-legged Aaron, age twelve, and four-legged Galaxy, nine.

This is how she came to adopt an amazing dog that nobody else wanted.

I was brought up around animals. Born in the sprawling desert of Las Vegas, I spent most of my time surrounded by dogs, cats, horses, and various reptiles. I like to think that being around animals my whole life gave me a distinct sense of comfort around them.

A shy and quiet child, I always felt a deeper bond with my animals than I ever did with kids my age. When the other kids were going to parties or hanging out under the bleachers, I was lying in the middle of a pasture with my horse, training my dogs, or cuddling with my cats.

Despite having no formal education in animal training, this upbringing helped teach me to understand animals uniquely. I've always been confident and sure of myself when handling animals. I always knew how to communicate with them and understand what they were communicating to me.

As an adult, I had to say goodbye to my childhood pets, and I lived pet free for a few years. I met my husband, Alan, and we had a beautiful child together. But while I adored my family, my home, and my life, something was always missing. So when our kid started asking for a dog, I loved the idea. But not even I could predict just how profoundly that new dog would change my life—and so many other lives!

Judy Katz is a book collaborator, ghostwriter, publisher, and marketer. Along with obtaining literary agents and publishers for her authors, she helps promote their books to serve them as the ultimate reputation-building tool. One recent project, *A Question of Respect: Bringing Us Together in a Deeply Divided Nation*, has garnered significant media attention and is a *Wall Street Journal* bestseller. An award-winning Holocaust memoir, *Angel of the Ghetto*, inspired a documentary. To date, she has completed sixty books. Judy also writes a regular column. These popular essays are intended to help change the conversation about aging.

A graduate of UC Berkeley, Judy wrote a weekly column, "Meaning's Edge," in the *Daily Californian* for all four years. She later wrote for a medical ad agency and two McGraw-Hill magazines before becoming PR director for Madison Square Garden and New York March of Dimes, and director of special projects for the National Multiple Sclerosis Society. At age sixty-five, Judy found her true calling when she began helping people become successful authors. Now eighty-five, she continues to pursue her mission, passion, and purpose. Judy is on LinkedIn and Facebook. She also just wrote a little autobiographic book, *From 18 to 84 and Counting: One Woman's Blueprint for a Joyous Third Act*, and coauthored this book with Jen Wilson. You can contact Judy at 917-841-1843, jkatzcreative@gmail.com, or www.katzcreativebooksandmedia.com.

www.ingramcontent.com/pod-product-compliance
Lightning Source LLC
Chambersburg PA
CBHW030322080526
44584CB00012B/667